RELATOS EN INGLÉS PARA EL VERANO

Edición: Grupo Vaughan
Maquetación: Fernando González
Ilustraciones: Guillermo Berdugo
Imprime: ROTÄBOOK

© Vaughan Systems S.L., 2015
C/ Orense 69, 1.a planta
28020 Madrid
Tel.: 91 444 58 44
Fax: 91 444 58 36
www.vaughantienda.com
Depósito Legal: B-17153-2015

Impreso en España / Printed in Spain

Introducción

55 episodes and their corresponding questions

Estimado amigo,

Quiero darle la bienvenida a la nueva reedición de la obra didáctica que más me ha gustado crear: *Relatos en inglés para el verano*. En realidad, esta nueva reedición es más que nada un simple cambio de diseño exterior, ya que los contenidos no necesitan ningún cambio por el momento. Los personajes siguen tan vivos como siempre y su vida milagros siguen sirviendo para introducir y practicar todas las formas y estructuras importantes del idioma inglés.

INTRODUCTION

Tengo un apego especial a estos personajes... curiosamente especial... ya que todos lograron en su día adquirir vida propia en mi esquema mental. De hecho, una de las mujeres sigue siendo, hoy por hoy, mi amor platónico más patente y perdurable, un amor que renuncié transformar en físico y material con la creación de un personaje secundario, de nacionalidad alemana, hombre serio, sensato y prudente que, al igual que yo, se queda perdidamente prendado de la joven y bella ejecutiva. Como ve, me cuesta renunciar a ella, así que si no la puedo tener yo, que sea un tipo en principio poco fascinante y poco seductor quien posiblemente la consiga.

Siguiendo por la estela de lo romántico, tenemos una sevillana, tan impetuosa como la Carmen de Bizet, cuya furia y viveza se quedan suspendidas, paradas en seco, por la imponente figura de un joven alto y rubio, de acento extraño, cuyo coche ella acaba de desgraciar al saltar un stop. Así de curiosa empieza una relación cuya desenlace incluye un piso en el barrio más bohemio de París.

Después está la mona y revoltosa alemanita que ingenuamente cae bajo la influencia de un americano de oscuros antecedentes. Estudiantes universitarios los dos, en la hermosa ciudad milenaria de Heidelberg, nuestra joven y simpática aspirante a diseñadora se ve obligada a usar todas sus artes para salir indemne del embrollo.

Oscuras intrigas también envuelven la vida y movimientos de un magnate inglés del mundo del espionaje privado, hombre que mientras resuelve casos de homicidios pasionales en Londres, organiza entre bastidores la forma de sacar a su descentrado hijo ligón, con domicilio en Monte Carlo, de una trama peligrosa con la mafia corsa.

Ya con más calma conocemos a la perfecta familia del medio oeste americano, tierra de trigo y maíz, familia de padre banquero, madre decoradora, hijo deportista e hija que transita entre la niñez y la adolescencia. Ahora bien, lo curioso de esta familia, tan convencional, es cómo llega a entrar en sus vidas un hombre de la fama de George Clooney. Entre campeonatos estatales de baloncesto y refinadas estaciones de esquí, esta familia acaba por tener una vida no tan convencional al final.

Otro personaje se ve en la tesitura de llevar a toda su familia desde la perfecta organización de una vida precisa y ordenada en Japón hasta una de las zonas más exóticas de la América profunda, Luisiana. Con hijos pequeños y una esposa de la más tradicional, nuestro ingeniero de calidad japonés tiene que someterse él y toda su familia a un cambio de 180 grados en sus vidas.

Después hay un empresario italiano de asientos de coche, una química rusa con ganas de conocer el mundo, un traductor del Ministerio de Asuntos Exteriores francés con acceso a documentos de los más secretos y comprometedores y un modesto obrero chino que logra lo imposible: alcanzar un alto dominio del inglés sin gastar casi tiempo ni dinero. Este último es la personificación de mis consejos de cómo aprender inglés por cuenta propia.

A través de las andanzas y peripecias de mis personajes, episodio tras episodio, el lector puede leer en las páginas del libro una creciente riqueza de sustantivos, verbos, adjetivos, adverbios, preposiciones y conjunciones, todo dentro de un estilo y una sintaxis cada vez más variados y exigentes. Al fin y al cabo, las historias interesantes de nuestros personajes no son más que un pretexto o, mejor dicho, un truco... una artimaña... para conseguir la atención del estudiante y ganar "cuota de mercado" en el tiempo que dedica a hacerse con el idioma inglés.

55 EPISODES
AND THEIR
CORRESPONDING
QUESTIONS

1. PHILLIP JOHNSON

Phillip Johnson is 39 years old. He's married and has two children. He lives in a nice house in Lincoln, Nebraska. He is a businessman and he works in a bank in the center of Lincoln. He is the General Manager of the bank. He goes to work every day at 8:30 in the morning. He gets to the office at 9:00. He parks his car under the bank in the parking garage. In the morning, he usually works from 9:00 to 12:30. He spends a lot of time talking on the telephone and reading financial reports. He usually has lunch near his office. There are many good restaurants in the center of Lincoln. He goes back to the office at 1:30 and stays there until 6:00. After work, he usually goes home, but sometimes he goes to his son's school to watch him play basketball or baseball. He usually gets home from work at 6:30, but when he goes to see his son, he gets home around 8:00. He likes his job because he has a good salary and because he works with a lot of interesting people. He doesn't travel very often in his job, but from time to time he needs to go to Omaha, a city 150 miles from Lincoln. When he goes to Omaha, he usually comes back to Lincoln on the same day, but sometimes he needs to spend the night there. He usually stays at the Omaha Sheraton Hotel, but sometimes he stays in the Holiday Inn. He prefers the Sheraton because it has a breakfast buffet.

1. PHILLIP JOHNSON

1. How old is Phillip?
2. Is he married or single?
3. Does he have any children?
4. How many children does he have?
5. Does he live in New York?
6. Where does he live?
7. Does he live in a nice house?
8. Is he an actor?
9. What does he do?
10. Does he work in a pharmacy?
11. Where does he work?
12. Is the bank outside of Lincoln?
13. Where is the bank?
14. Does he have an important job?
15. What's his position in the bank?
16. Does he go to work every day?
17. What time does he go to work?
18. Does he get to the office at 8:45?
19. What time does he get to the office?
20. Does he park in the street?
21. Where does he park?
22. How long does he work in the morning?
23. Does he spend a lot of time with customers?
24. What does he spend a lot of time doing?
25. Does he have lunch at home?
26. Where does he usually have lunch?
27. Are there many good restaurants near his office?
28. What time does he go back to the office after lunch?
29. Does he stay at the office until 7 o'clock?
30. How long does he stay at the office?
31. Does he go to a bar with his friends after work?
32. Where does he usually go after work?
33. What time does he usually get home?
34. Does he always go home after work?
35. Where does he sometimes go?
36. Why does he go to his son's school?
37. What time does he get home when he's with his son?
38. Does he like his job?
39. Why does he like it?
40. Does he often travel in his job?
41. Where does he need to go from time to time?
42. How far is Omaha from Lincoln?
43. Does he usually stay in Omaha for several days?
44. How long does he usually stay in Omaha?
45. Does he always spend the night in Omaha?
46. Does he usually stay at the Palace Hotel in Omaha?
47. Where does he usually stay?
48. Where does he sometimes stay?
49. Which hotel does he prefer?
50. Why does he prefer it?

Nancy Johnson is 38 years old. She is Phillip's wife. She lives with her husband and children in Lincoln, Nebraska. She's from Kansas, the state immediately south of Nebraska. She is an interior decorator. In the morning, she teaches interior design at a technical school 20 miles from Lincoln. She starts her classes every day at 10:00 and finishes at 12:00. She has two classes, each with about 15 students. Then she goes home to have lunch. After lunch, she goes to her husband's bank where she spends about 30 minutes with the woman responsible for expansion. She looks at the plans for the new bank branches and gives recommendations about the interior design and decoration. She doesn't receive a salary for this. She does it because the woman is a good friend of hers. In the afternoon, she works as an independent decorator. Some days, she spends two or three hours visiting different clients and other days she stays at home creating decoration plans or calling people. She decorates offices, restaurants and homes. She doesn't like to decorate offices very much because the companies usually prefer functional decoration and this is boring for her. She doesn't like to decorate restaurants either, because often the owner of the restaurant thinks that he's a professional decorator too. She likes to decorate homes because she is free to make more decisions and to be more creative.

2. NANCY JOHNSON

1. Is Nancy 33 years old?
2. How old is she?
3. Is she Nigel's wife?
4. Whose wife is she?
5. Who does she live with?
6. Where does she live?
7. Is she from Nebraska?
8. Where is she from?
9. Is Kansas far from Nebraska?
10. Is it near Nebraska?
11. Is it north or south of Nebraska?
12. Is Nancy a school teacher?
13. What does she do?
14. Does she teach?
15. What does she teach?
16. Does she teach interior design in the evenings?
17. When does she teach it?
18. Does she teach it at a university?
19. Where does she teach it?
20. Is the technical school in the center of Lincoln?
21. Where is it?
22. How many days a week does she teach?
23. What time does she start her classes?
24. What time does she finish?
25. Does she have three classes?
26. How many classes does she have?
27. Are there 20 students in each class?
28. How many students are there in each class?
29. Does she have lunch near the technical school?
30. Where does she have lunch?
31. Does she stay at home after lunch?
32. Where does she go after lunch?
33. Does she stay at the bank all afternoon?
34. Does she spend an hour there every day?
35. How much time does she spend at the bank?
36. Does she spend this time with her husband?
37. Who does she spend the time with?
38. What is this woman responsible for?
39. Does Nancy help this woman?
40. What kind of plans does she look at?
41. Does she give recommendations?
42. What kind of recommendations does she give?
43. Does she receive a nice salary for this help?
44. How much money does she receive?
45. Does she help the woman because she's bored?
46. Why does she help the woman?
47. What does Nancy do in the afternoon?
48. Does she work in an office?
49. Where does she work when she's not visiting clients?
50. What does she do when she is working at home?
51. Does she visit her clients every day?
52. How often does she visit clients?
53. Does she only decorate homes?
54. What kind of places does she decorate?
55. Does she like to decorate offices?
56. Why not?
57. Does she like to decorate restaurants?
58. Why not?
59. Does she like to decorate homes?
60. Why does she like to decorate homes?

3. MICHAEL JOHNSON

Michael Johnson is 14 years old. He lives with his parents and sister in Lincoln, Nebraska. He goes to a public school 10 minutes from his house by car. His sister goes to a different school three blocks from his. Michael is in the ninth grade and he studies Math, Science, History, English, Speech and Music. He plays the trumpet in music class, but he isn't a member of the school band because he doesn't have time to practice with the band after school. School starts at 9 o'clock. Michael gets to school a little early because his father takes him every day and leaves him there at 8:40. Michael spends the 20 minutes before his first class talking with some of his friends. Lunch is at 12:00 and Michael usually eats a sandwich and a bowl of soup and drinks a Coke. His mother doesn't like this, so Michael tells his mother that he drinks milk for lunch. His classes in the afternoon end at 3:30. Michael is a member of the football, basketball and baseball teams at school. He is a good athlete. He's fast and strong. He plays football in the fall, between September and December. He plays basketball in the winter, between January and April, and he plays baseball in the spring. He is a very popular boy because he is good at sports. He's intelligent but he doesn't work very hard in class and he doesn't spend much time on his homework. His teachers like him but they tell his parents that he needs to think more about his studies and less about sports.

3. MICHAEL JOHNSON

1. Is Michael 12 years old?
2. How old is he?
3. Does he live alone?
4. Who does he live with?
5. Does he live in Kansas?
6. Where does he live?
7. Does he go to a private school?
8. What kind of school does he go to?
9. Is the school far from his house?
10. Is it near or far from his house?
11. How far is it from his house by car?
12. Does his sister go to the same school?
13. Does she go to the same school or to a different one?
14. Is his school far from his sister's school?
15. How far is it from his sister's school?
16. Is Michael in the 8th grade?
17. What grade is he in?
18. Does he study just 3 subjects?
19. How many subjects does he study?
20. Does he study Speech and Music?
21. What other 4 subjects does he study?
22. Does he play a musical instrument in music class?
23. Does he play the clarinet?
24. What instrument does he play?
25. Is he a member of the school band?
26. Why not?
27. Does the band practice before school?
28. When does the band practice?
29. Does school start at 9:30?
30. What time does school start?
31. Does Michael often get to school late?
32. When does he get to school?
33. Why does he get to school a little early?
34. How often does his father take him to school?
35. Does his father leave him at school at 8:30?
36. What time does his father leave him at school?
37. Does Michael spend the 20 minutes studying?
38. What does he spend the time doing?
39. Does he have lunch at home?
40. Where does he have lunch?
41. Does he have lunch at 12:30?
42. What time does he have lunch?
43. Does Michael usually eat a sandwich at school?
44. What else does he eat?
45. Does he drink milk for lunch?
46. Does he drink Pepsi Cola?
47. What does he drink?
48. Does his mother know that he drinks Coke?
49. What does she think he drinks?
50. Why does she think he drinks milk?
51. Does Michael have classes after lunch?
52. What time does he finish school?
53. Does Michael like sports?
54. Is he a good athlete or a bad athlete?
55. Does he play any sports at school?
56. How many sports does he play?
57. Does he play basketball?
58. What other two sports does he play?
59. Is he a member of the school team in these sports?
60. Is he fast and strong?
61. When does he play football?
62. When does he play basketball?
63. When does he play baseball?
64. Is he a popular boy at school?
65. Why is he popular?
66. Is he an intelligent boy?
67. Is he a good student?
68. Why isn't he a good student?
69. Do his teachers like him?
70. What do they tell his parents?

4. DENISE JOHNSON

Denise Johnson is 11 years old. She lives with her parents and brother in Lincoln, Nebraska. She goes to a primary school near her brother's school. She is in her last year of primary school. Her father takes her to school every day with her brother. She gets to school at 8:45 and goes to the playground to play with her friends. Her first class begins at 9:00. She has the same teacher all morning, until 12:00. Then she has lunch in the school cafeteria. She always eats with her two friends, Jenny and Pamela. They live on the same block and study in the same class. They spend more than six hours together at school and probably three or four hours together after school. Denise's mother likes Jenny but she doesn't like Pamela very much. She thinks Pamela is very bossy. Two days a week, Denise stays after school in the gym for ballet classes. She doesn't have a natural talent for ballet, but she likes to dance and has a very good technique. The teacher thinks that she has the potential to become a good dancer, especially if she doesn't grow too fast. On the days that Denise has ballet, she stays at the school until 4:30. Jenny takes ballet lessons too, and Jenny's mother takes both of them home after the lessons.

4. DENISE JOHNSON

1. How old is Denise Johnson?
2. Who does she live with?
3. Does she live in Omaha?
4. Where does she live?
5. Does she attend a secondary school?
6. What kind of school does she attend?
7. Is she in her first year?
8. What year is she in?
9. Does she go to school on the bus?
10. How does she go to school?
11. Does she get to school at 9:00?
12. What time does she get to school?
13. Does she study before her first class begins?
14. Where does she go when she gets to school?
15. Does she play with her brother in the playground?
16. Who does she play with in the playground?
17. Does her first class begin at 8:45?
18. What time does it begin?
19. Does she have 5 teachers during the morning?
20. How many teachers does she have in the morning?
21. Does she have this teacher all day?
22. How long does she have this teacher?
23. Does she have lunch at 11:30?
24. What time does she have lunch?
25. Does she go home for lunch?
26. Where does she have lunch?
27. Does she eat with her brother?
28. Who does she eat with?
29. Does she always eat with the same friends?
30. What are their names?
31. Do the friends spend a lot of time together?
32. How many hours do the friends spend together?
33. Does Denise's mother like Jenny?
34. What is her opinion of Pamela?
35. Does she think Pamela is introverted?
36. Why doesn't she like Pamela?
37. Does Denise go home after school every day?
38. What does she sometimes do after school?
39. How often does she stay after school?
40. Where does she take the ballet lessons?
41. Does Denise have a natural talent for ballet?
42. Does she like to dance?
43. What is her strong point in ballet?
44. What does the ballet teacher think about Denise?
45. What time does Denise finish her ballet lessons?
46. Does Pamela take lessons too?
47. Which friend takes ballet lessons with Denise?
48. Does Denise's mother take her home after the class?
49. Does she go home alone?
50. How does she go home from the ballet class?

5. NIGEL PERKINS

Nigel Perkins is 55 years old. He's English and lives on a country estate 35 miles north of London near the M-1 motorway. He's married to Margaret Perkins and has one son, Ronny. Nigel owns a company that investigates suspicious people who receive big payments from insurance companies. His company is very famous in the United Kingdom and it has a lot of important clients. It even has some clients in France and in the United States. Nigel doesn't work every day. He goes to the office in the center of London two or three times a week. He has a good team of managers who run the company very well. On the days that Nigel doesn't go to London, he likes to spend his time reading and taking care of his garden. His estate is big. It covers almost 30,000 square meters. Nigel has three full-time gardeners to help him to take care of the estate. Nigel wants to write a book about some of the interesting investigations from his company's past. He thinks that one or two of the investigations are good material for a novel or even for a suspense movie. His son, Ronny, thinks he's crazy, but Nigel doesn't pay any attention to his son. Ronny spends his time on the French Riviera, where he owns a small company that rents yachts for short cruises between Monte Carlo and the Balearic Islands. He makes a lot of money in the summer and asks his father for money in the winter.

5. NIGEL PERKINS

1. How old is Nigel Perkins?
2. Is he American?
3. What nationality is he?
4. Does he live in France?
5. What country does he live in?
6. Does he live in London?
7. Does he live north or south of London?
8. How far north of London does he live?
9. Does he live near or far from the motorway?
10. Which motorway does he live near?
11. Does he live in an apartment or on a country estate?
12. Is he married or single?
13. Who is he married to?
14. How many children does he have?
15. What's his son's name?
16. Does Nigel work for a company or own a company?
17. What kind of people does his company investigate?
18. Is Nigel's company famous?
19. Does it have many clients?
20. Are the majority of its clients from the U.K.?
21. Where does it have clients outside of the U.K.?
22. Does Nigel go to the office every day?
23. How often does he go to the office?
24. Is the office near his estate?
25. Where is it?
26. Does Nigel have a good team of managers?
27. How do they run the company?
28. What does Nigel do when he doesn't go to his office?
29. Is his estate big?
30. How many square meters does it cover?
31. Does Nigel need gardeners for his estate?
32. How many gardeners does he need?
33. Do the gardeners work part-time or full-time?
34. Does Nigel want to start a new company in the U.S.?
35. Does he want to write?
36. What does he want to write?
37. What does he want to write a book about?
38. What does he think about one or two investigations?
39. What does Ronny think about this?
40. How does Nigel react to Ronny's opinion?
41. Does Ronny live with his parents?
42. Where does he live?
43. Does he work in a bank?
44. What does he own?
45. What does the company rent?
46. Where do the yachts go from Monte Carlo?
47. Does Ronny make a lot of money?
48. What part of the year does he make the money?
49. Does he make a lot of money in the winter?
50. How does he get money in the winter?

6. LUIGI BARGHINI

Luigi Barghini is 49 years old. He's from a small town in the north of Italy and now lives with his wife, Sofia, in a beautiful villa outside Verona. He has a lot of money because he owns a big factory that supplies car seats to Fiat in Turin. Luigi is the Chairman of the company, but his daughter, Anna, is the Managing Director. She takes care of the day-to-day business, while Luigi spends a lot of his time visiting different members of the Agnelli family that owns Fiat. He also spends a lot of time in Germany, because his company is negotiating a big contract with Mercedes Benz to supply car seats for the small models that Mercedes makes in Stuttgart. He is a very busy man, but he enjoys his work. When he's at his villa near Verona, he always goes to the factory, 23 kilometers away, to see his daughter and to visit the workers. He probably spends at least three hours on the floor of the factory talking with workers, inviting them to coffee, telling jokes and having a good time. He likes the people in the north of Italy and really enjoys human contact. That's probably the reason why his company is strong and healthy. He doesn't consider that his work is a job. He considers it a game, something that he likes to play. Of course, he wants to win and he wins, but he has a good disposition all the time and he doesn't like to take things too seriously. His daughter, Anna, is different, but she is a manager, not an owner.

6. LUIGI BARGHINI

1. How old is Luigi Barghini?
2. Is he from a big city or a small town?
3. Where is the small town?
4. Where does he live now?
5. Does he live in a beautiful villa or a small flat?
6. Who does he live with?
7. What's his wife's name?
8. Does Luigi have a lot of money or only a little money?
9. Why does he have a lot of money?
10. What does the factory supply to Fiat?
11. Where is Fiat?
12. What is Luigi's position in his company?
13. Who is the Managing Director of his company?
14. What does she take care of in the company?
15. What does Luigi spend a lot of time doing?
16. What other country does he spend time visiting?
17. What company does he visit in Germany?
18. What is he negotiating with Mercedes Benz?
19. Are the car seats for small or big models?
20. Where does Mercedes make its small models?
21. Is Luigi a busy man?
22. How does he feel about his work?
23. When he's not traveling, does he stay at home?
24. Where does he go every day when he's at his villa?
25. How far is the factory from his villa?
26. Does he see his daughter when he goes there?
27. Who else does he visit at the factory?
28. How many hours does he spend with the workers?
29. What does he invite the workers to?
30. What does he tell them?
31. Does he like the people in the north of Italy?
32. What does he enjoy?
33. Why is his company strong and healthy?
34. Does he consider his work a job or a game?
35. Does he like to win?
36. What kind of disposition does he have?
37. Does he take things too seriously?
38. Is his daughter similar to him?
39. Why is she different?

7. PIERRE MONET

Pierre Monet is 45 years old and lives in the suburbs of Paris. He is married and has three children. All of his children live at home except Gerard, who lives in a student hall of residence not far from the Sorbonne, where he studies architecture. Pierre is a civil servant. He works in the translation and interpretation department of the Foreign Ministry in the center of Paris. Every day he goes by train and subway from his house outside of Paris to the Ministry. It takes him almost an hour to go and about 45 minutes to come back in the afternoon. He leaves home at 7:00 and gets to the Ministry just before 8:00. When he gets to his office, he always has a lot of letters and documents waiting for him. He is responsible for a very special area of his department. He decodes and translates all secret documents that come in English and Spanish. He speaks and writes both languages fluently. His wife is Spanish and his mother is English. Pierre is an expert translator. He doesn't usually translate documents in writing. He verbally dictates the translation directly into a microphone. Later, a secretary transcribes the recording onto paper. This way, Pierre translates very quickly and finishes his work early. He usually goes home around 4:00 p.m. He doesn't have lunch in the dining hall of the Ministry. He takes a sandwich to work every day and eats it at 12 o'clock sharp. He prefers to continue his work without interruptions in order to go home as early as possible. When he gets home, he starts his second job. He is a freelance translator and he dictates his translations into his own microphone. The same evening, or the next morning, his wife, Anne-Marie, enters the recording into a computer and sends it by e-mail to Pierre's clients. Pierre has a good salary at the Ministry, but he earns double at home. He needs the money because his three children are very intelligent and all of them want to go to university.

7. PIERRE MONET

1. How old is Pierre Monet?
2. Does he live in Paris or London?
3. Where does he live in Paris?
4. Is he married or single?
5. How many children does he have?
6. How many of his children live at home?
7. Where does his son, Gerard, live?
8. Is the residence near or far from the Sorbonne?
9. What does Gerard study at the Sorbonne?
10. Does Pierre work in a company?
11. Is he a civil servant or a politician?
12. What Ministry does he work in?
13. What department does he work in?
14. Where is the Foreign Ministry?
15. Does Pierre drive to work every day?
16. 16. How does he go to work?
17. Does it take him two hours to go to work?
18. How long does it take him?
19. How long does it take him to go back home?
20. What time does he leave home in the morning?
21. What time does he get to the Ministry?
22. What does he have waiting for him at the office?
23. What kind of area is he responsible for?
24. What kind of documents does he translate?
25. What languages does he speak fluently?
26. Why does he speak Spanish fluently?
27. Why does he speak English fluently?
28. Is Pierre an expert translator?
29. Does he usually translate documents in writing?
30. How does he translate them?
31. Later, does Pierre transcribe the recordings?
32. Who transcribes them?
33. Why does Pierre use this method of translation?
34. Does Pierre often finish work late?
35. Does he usually finish late or early?
36. What time does he usually go home?
37. Does he have lunch in the dining hall at the Ministry?
38. Why doesn't he have lunch in the dining hall?
39. What time does he eat his sandwich?
40. Why does he prefer to work without interruptions?
41. What does he start when he gets home?
42. What is his second job?
43. How does he translate at home?
44. What's his wife's name?
45. What does she do with her husband's recordings?
46. When does she do this?
47. How does she send the translations to the clients?
48. What kind of salary does Pierre have at the Ministry?
49. How much does he earn at home?
50. Why does he need more money?

8. PAULA EISENBACH

Paula Eisenbach is 22 years old. She is in her last year at the University of Heidelberg, where she is studying computer systems and graphic arts. She is from Munich, in the south of Germany. Heidelberg is a town in Germany famous for its beauty and for its university. Paula likes it very much. She lives in a flat with two other friends. One of them studies graphic arts too, and the other works in a fashion shop in the center of the town. Paula spends all of her time attending classes, doing homework, and helping Tom, an American student who lives near her in Heidelberg. Tom is studying graphic arts too, but he is also working part-time for the Walt Disney Corporation as an artist for Disney cartoons. Tom receives a lot of instructions from the Disney people in California over the Internet. With these instructions, he draws the cartoon characters and scenes and sends them back to California by computer. Disney sends him a lot of work and he gives some of it to Paula. Paula helps him in the evenings and sometimes on the weekends. She likes the artistic work because she wants to improve her technique. She likes to draw, and she's very artistic, but she doesn't have the patience or discipline to spend a long time developing complicated scenes or characters. Tom is the opposite and Paula is learning a lot by working with him. They are very good friends. Tom is from California and he wants to go back for the Christmas holidays. He wants to invite Paula to go with him. She's not sure because she doesn't know Tom very well yet.

8. PAULA EISENBACH

1. Is Paula Eisenbach 40 years old?
2. How old is she?
3. Does she live in Frankfurt?
4. Where does she live?
5. Does she live there because she works there?
6. Why does she live in Heidelberg?
7. What is she studying at the university?
8. Is she from Heidelberg?
9. Where's she from?
10. Where's Munich?
11. Is Heidelberg famous for its beer?
12. What is Heidelberg famous for?
13. Does Paula like Heidelberg?
14. Does she live in a house or in a flat?
15. Does she live alone?
16. Who does she live with?
17. What does one of the friends study?
18. Is the other friend a student too?
19. Is she a fashion model?
20. Where does she work?
21. Where's the shop?
22. What does Paula spend all of her time doing?
23. What country is Tom from?
24. Is he a student?
25. Does he live outside of Heidelberg?
26. Where does he live?
27. What is he studying?
28. Who does he work for part-time?
29. What does he draw for the Disney Corporation?
30. Who does he receive instructions from?
31. Does he receive the instructions by telephone?
32. How does he receive them?
33. How does he send the drawings back to California?
34. Does Tom do all the work alone?
35. Who helps him?
36. When does she help him?
37. Does she like this work?
38. Why does she like it?
39. Is she artistic?
40. Does she like to spend a long time drawing?
41. Why not?
42. Is Tom similar to Paula in this respect?
43. Is Paula learning a lot from Tom?
44. What is their relationship?
45. Where is Tom from in the U.S.?
46. When does he want to go back?
47. Does he want to go back alone?
48. Who does he want to invite?
49. Does Paula want to go?
50. What's the problem?

Li Tong is 36 years old. He lives in a small apartment with his wife and young daughter in Shanghai, a city with a population of 15 million people. He works in a factory near the port that makes telephones for the big demand that exists in the new China. Li's apartment is very small. He and his wife sleep in the one bedroom and their daughter sleeps on a small bed in the living room. Li's factory is doing very well and Li's salary is increasing. Now he has a television, a telephone and a washing machine. His wife wants to work and she is looking for a job. His daughter goes to a public school every day near their house. Her grandfather comes to the house at 8:30 every morning and takes her to school. He takes her home again at 1o'clock for lunch and takes her back to school at 2:00. Her last class ends at 5:00 and her grandfather takes her home again. The grandfather has lunch with his granddaughter every day. Li goes to work every day by bicycle. He leaves home at 5 o'clock in the morning. It takes him almost an hour to get to the factory. He works there from 6:00 a.m. to 2:00 p.m. He gets back home at 3:00. He takes some food to work every morning. His wife prepares the food the night before and puts it in Li's shoulder bag. He usually eats a chicken sandwich, but sometimes his wife doesn't have any chicken. In these cases, she prepares tofu, a popular food made from soy beans. Li lives relatively well in comparison with the majority of the people in Shanghai. He is a member of the new middle class that is starting to appear in China.

9. LI TONG

1. Is Li Tong 31 years old?
2. How old is he?
3. Does he live in Peking?
4. What city does he live in?
5. Does he live in a small apartment or in a big house?
6. Does he live with his mother?
7. Who does he live with?
8. Is Shanghai a big city or a small city?
9. Are there 20 million people in Shanghai?
10. How many people are there in Shanghai?
11. Does Li Tong work in an office?
12. Where does he work?
13. Is the factory near the mountains?
14. What is the factory near?
15. Does the factory make shoes?
16. What does it make?
17. Is there a big demand for telephones in China?
18. Is Li's apartment big or small?
19. Does it have three bedrooms?
20. How many bedrooms does it have?
21. Who sleeps in the bedroom?
22. What room does Li's daughter sleep in?
23. How is Li's factory doing?
24. What is the situation concerning his salary?
25. What three new things does Li have at home?
26. Does his wife have a job?
27. Does she want to work?
28. What is she looking for?
29. Does Li's daughter go to a public or private school?
30. Is the school near or far from Li's house?
31. Who takes Li's daughter to school every day?
32. What time does the grandfather get to Li's house?
33. What time does he take Li's daughter home?
34. Why does he take her home at 1 o'clock?
35. What time does he take her back to school?
36. Does Li's daughter stay at school until 7:00 p.m.?
37. What time does she finish school?
38. Where does the grandfather have lunch every day?
39. Who does he have lunch with?
40. Does Li go to work by bus?
41. How does he go to work?
42. Does it take him 30 minutes to get to work?
43. How long does it take him?
44. What time does he start work?
45. What time does he finish?
46. How long does he stay in the factory?
47. What time does he get home?
48. Does he have lunch at home?
49. Where does he have lunch?
50. Does he have lunch in the factory canteen?
51. Who prepares his lunch for him?
52. When does she prepare it?
53. Where does she put the sandwich?
54. What does Li usually eat?
55. Why doesn't he eat a chicken sandwich every time?
56. What does his wife do when there isn't any chicken?
57. What is tofu?
58. How does Li live in comparison to other people?
59. Is he a member of the lower class?
60. What class is he a member of?

Aki Morita is 39 years old. He is a member of the group of young executives at Honda that want to have an influence on the future of the company. He is an engineer, but he doesn't work in an engineering job. He is the manager of the department for quality analysis. This means counting all the parts and components in the factory that have a defect. Aki really doesn't have to count many defects because he and his people spend a lot of time visiting Honda's suppliers. Honda has a strict quality manual which Aki gives to every new supplier who works for the company. After this, he and his people spend about 50 % of their time with the new supplier, watching the process and finding ways to make it better. Aki's department is probably responsible for the excellent quality record at Honda and Aki knows that his bosses know this. He has a very good salary and lives in a nice area of Osaka, an industrial city south of Tokyo. He has a wife and two children, but he doesn't see them very often because he works 14 hours every day and 5 or 6 hours on Saturday. He doesn't like to work so many hours, but he thinks that this is the only way to move up in the organization and pay for the expensive private school where he sends his children. His wife doesn't say anything about the hours that her husband works. In fact, she prefers the situation because it gives her a lot of money to go shopping and to take care of the children.

10. AKI MORITA

1. How old is Aki Morita?
2. Does he work for Toyota?
3. What company does he work for?
4. Is he a factory worker?
5. Is he an executive?
6. Is he a young executive or an old executive?
7. Is he a member of a group of young executives?
8. What does this group want to do at Honda?
9. Is Aki a lawyer?
10. What does he do?
11. Does he work in an engineering job?
12. What department is he the manager of?
13. What does this department do?
14. Are there many defects in the parts and components?
15. Why not?
16. What does Aki give to Honda suppliers?
17. How much time does Aki spend with new suppliers?
18. What does he do in the suppliers' factories?
19. What is Aki's department probably responsible for?
20. Do the bosses at Honda know about Aki's work?
21. Does Aki know that they know?
22. What about Aki's salary?
23. Does Aki live in Tokyo?
24. What city does he live in?
25. What kind of area in Osaka does he live in?
26. Is Osaka a commercial city or an industrial city?
27. Where is Osaka in relation to Tokyo?
28. Who does Aki live with?
29. Does he see them very often?
30. Why not?
31. How many hours does he work every week?
32. Does he like to work so many hours?
33. Does he want to work less?
34. Why does he want to continue working so much?
35. Does he send his children to a public school?
36. What kind of school does he send them to?
37. Is the school cheap or expensive?
38. Does his wife complain about the hours Aki works?
39. What is her opinion about the situation?
40. Why does she prefer the situation?

11. NATASHA ZARAKOVICH

Natasha Zarakovich is 28 years old. She lives with her mother and brother in a small apartment near Gorky Park in Moscow. She is a chemist and works in the Russian State Laboratory which analyzes and gives approval to pharmaceutical drugs that Russian laboratories produce or that foreign companies want to sell in Russia. She likes her job because she has a good salary and the laboratory is not far from her house. She goes to work every morning on the subway. The laboratory is only three subway stops away from her house and she usually reads novels in English on the way to work. She wants to improve her English because she has a cousin who lives in Scotland. Her cousin invites Natasha to visit him in Scotland every year, but Natasha doesn't have enough money to go. She wants to go next year, but she's not sure yet. Every day Natasha starts work in the laboratory at 7:30 in the morning. She prefers to begin early because there are fewer people in the subway at that time. She works continuously in the lab until 12:00, when she goes home to have lunch with her mother. She gets back to the lab at 1:30 and continues until 4:30. Sometimes she stays past 4:30 if her boss needs her help, but usually she goes to the national library, near the laboratory, and reads until 6:30 or 7:00. Her house is small and noisy, especially when her brother and his friends are there, and she prefers the quiet and solitude of the library. She always reads in English because she wants to take the State English Examination. If she passes it, she automatically receives an increase in her salary.

11. NATASHA ZARAKOVICH

1. How old is Natasha Zarakovich?
2. Who does she live with?
3. Does she live in a big or small apartment?
4. Does she live in St. Petersburg?
5. What city does she live in?
6. Does she live near the Kremlin?
7. What does she live near?
8. What does she do?
9. Does she work for a private company?
10. Where does she work?
11. What kind of drugs does the laboratory analyze?
12. Does it analyze drugs from foreign companies?
13. Does Natasha like her job?
14. 14. What about her salary?
15. Is the laboratory near or far from her house?
16. Does Natasha go to work by bus?
17. How does she go to work?
18. How many stops is the laboratory from her house?
19. Does Natasha read the newspaper on the subway?
20. What does she usually read?
21. What kind of novels does she read?
22. Why does she read English novels?
23. Why does she want to improve her English?
24. How often does her cousin invite her to Scotland?
25. Does she go?
26. Why doesn't she go to Scotland?
27. Does she want to go?
28. When does she want to go?
29. What time does she start work every day?
30. Does she prefer to go to work early?
31. Why does she prefer this?
32. How many breaks does she take during the morning?
33. Does she have lunch in the laboratory?
34. Where does she have lunch?
35. What time does she go home for lunch?
36. Who does she have lunch with?
37. What time does she get back to the lab?
38. What time does she finish work?
39. Does she always leave work at 4:30?
40. Why does she sometimes stay later?
41. Where does she usually go after work?
42. Is the library near or far from the laboratory?
43. Until what time does she stay at the library?
44. Does she like to go home to read and study?
45. Why not?
46. When is the house particularly noisy?
47. Why does she like the library?
48. What language does she read in?
49. What kind of examination does she want to take?
50. What does she receive if she passes the exam?

12. INÉS GARCÍA

Inés García is 24 years old. She lives with her parents about 20 kilometers east of Seville, in the south of Spain. She is a lawyer and works in her father's law firm in the center of Seville. This is her first year in the firm and she does a lot of the jobs that the other lawyers don't like to do. She knows how to use computers well and the other lawyers and secretaries in the office always ask her for help. She doesn't mind helping them, but sometimes she gets the impression that they are taking advantage of her. She also works on some of the legal cases that other lawyers don't want to handle. She spends a lot of time at the court defending labor cases. Her father's law firm has a lot of big companies as clients and Inés spends a lot of time preparing cases concerning labor disputes. Her father says that it's good experience and Inés agrees. She prepares the cases very well, but she doesn't want to work in the area of labor law for many years. In the future, she wants to work in mergers and acquisitions, where one company buys another company or two companies join to create a new one. She likes this area of law because it includes a lot of financial aspects which she is studying now at night on a special course that she is taking in business management and finance at the University of Seville. She goes there three nights a week from 6:00 p.m. to 9:00 p.m.

12. INÉS GARCÍA

1. How old is Inés?
2. Who does she live with?
3. Does she live in the north or south of Spain?
4. What city does she live in?
5. Does she live in Seville or outside of Seville?
6. How far does she live from Seville?
7. Does she live 20 kilometers east or west of Seville?
8. Is she a doctor?
9. What does she do?
10. Does she work in the public sector?
11. Does she work in a law firm?
12. Whose law firm does she work in?
13. Is this her first or second year in the law firm?
14. Does she do a lot of different things in the firm?
15. What kind of things does she do?
16. Why do other people in the firm ask her for help?
17. Does she mind helping them?
18. What kind of impression does she get sometimes?
19. What kind of legal cases does she work with?
20. Where does she spend a lot of time?
21. What kind of legal cases does she defend?
22. What kind of clients does her father's law firm have?
23. What kind of cases does Inés spend time preparing?
24. What does her father say about this?
25. Does Inés agree with her father?
26. How does she prepare the cases?
27. Does she want to work with labor cases for long?
28. What does she want to work with in the future?
29. What is an acquisition?
30. What is a merger?
31. Why does she like this area of law?
32. Is she taking a special course now?
33. What course is she taking?
34. Where does she attend the class?
35. When does the class take place?
36. Does she go there every night?
37. How many nights a week does she go there?
38. How long does the class last?
39. What time does it begin?
40. What time does it end?

13. PHILLIP JOHNSON

Yesterday, Phillip Johnson had a busy mor - ning. He usually gets up at 7:30 every morning, but yesterday he got up at 7:00 because his wife, Nancy, had to leave home very early to take a report to a client of hers 70 miles from Lincoln. Nancy left home at 7:25 and Phillip made break- fast for himself and for the children. Usually Nancy makes breakfast for all three, but yesterday was an exception. Phillip took a shower and had breakfast before the children got up. He prepared fried eggs and toast for Michael and Denise and at 8:30 he took them to school. He got to the of- fice at ten minutes past nine. He had three meetings during the morning. The first one was at 10 o'clock with the bank's lawyer. They discussed a problem with an important client who wanted to suspend payments on a loan. They decided to wait until the meeting of the bank's Board of Direc- tors to make a final decision. At 11:30, he received the owner of a ceramic factory near Lincoln. The man needed $500,000 to add a new building to his factory. The ceramic factory was one of the best in Nebraska and Phillip knew the man very well and trusted him. At 12:00, Phillip met with the chief commercial officer of the bank to discuss a salary ques- tion concerning one of the employees in the commercial department. He went to lunch with the chief commercial officer at 12:30. They had lunch in a small restaurant near the office.

13. PHILLIP JOHNSON

1. Did Phillip have a busy morning yesterday?
2. Did he get up at the usual time?
3. What time did he get up?
4. What time does he usually get up?
5. Why did he get up earlier than usual?
6. Why did Nancy have to leave home early?
7. How far was the client from Lincoln?
8. What time did Nancy leave home?
9. Who prepared breakfast for Phillip?
10. Who usually makes breakfast?
11. Was yesterday an exception?
12. What did Phillip do before the children got up?
13. What did he prepare his children for breakfast?
14. What time did he leave home?
15. Did he leave home alone?
16. Who did he leave home with?
17. Why did he leave home with his children?
18. What time did he get to the office?
19. Did he have any meetings during the morning?
20. How many meetings did he have?
21. Was the first meeting at 9:30?
22. What time was the first meeting?
23. Was the meeting with a salesman?
24. Who was the first meeting with?
25. Did they discuss a problem?
26. What was the problem?
27. Did they make a final decision during the meeting?
28. What did they decide to do?
29. What time was his second meeting?
30. Who did Phillip receive?
31. How much money did the man need?
32. What did he need the money for?
33. What can you say about the ceramic factory?
34. What was Phillip's relationship with the man?
35. Who did Phillip meet with at 12 o'clock?
36. What did they discuss?
37. How long did the meeting last?
38. What time did Phillip go to lunch?
39. Who did he have lunch with?
40. Where did they have lunch?

Yesterday morning wasn't a normal morning for Nancy Johnson. She usually gets up at 7:30, but yesterday she got up at 6:30. She took a shower, got dressed, and had breakfast in less than 45 minutes. She left home at 7:25 because she had to drive 70 miles to the west of Lincoln to deliver an interior design plan to John Evans, the owner of a house that she is decorating. Mr. Evans needed to give the plan to the company that is building a new master bedroom for him and his wife. Nancy had to deliver it early in the morning because she didn't have any time the rest of the day to drive to Mr. Evans' house. Her problem was that she had to be at the technical school where she teaches interior design at 10 o'clock, when her first class started. The technical school is 20 miles east of Lincoln, so Nancy had to drive a total of 160 miles before 10:00. She drove relatively fast and got to Mr. Evans' house at 8:35. She spent ten minutes talking to him about some details of the plan and then started her drive to the school at 8:45. She had to drive 90 miles in an hour and fifteen minutes. Fortunately, Lincoln is a relatively small city and there isn't a lot of traffic. She got to the school at exactly five minutes to ten. She had a quick coffee with one of the other teachers and entered her class at two minutes past ten.

14. NANCY JOHNSON

1. Did Nancy have a normal morning yesterday?
2. What time does she usually get up?
3. What time did she get up yesterday?
4. What did she do before having breakfast?
5. What time did she leave home?
6. How far did she have to drive to Mr. Evans' house?
7. Is the house east or west of Lincoln?
8. What did she have to deliver to Mr. Evans?
9. Who is Mr Evans?
10. What is he doing with his house?
11. Who is the new bedroom for?
12. Who did he need to give the design plan to?
13. Why didn't Nancy deliver the plan later in the day?
14. What time did she have to be at the technical school?
15. How far is the technical school from Lincoln?
16. How far is it from Mr. Evans' house?
17. Explain why she had to drive 160 miles yesterday.
18. Why did Nancy have to be at the school at 10:00?
19. Did she drive relatively fast or slowly?
20. What time did she get to Mr. Evans' house?
21. How much time did she spend talking to him?
22. What did she talk to him about?
23. What time did she leave Mr. Evans' house?
24. How long was the trip to the school?
25. Was there a lot of traffic?
26. Why wasn't there a lot of traffic?
27. What time did Nancy get to the school?
28. What did she have before going to her class?
29. Who did she have a coffee with?
30. What time did she enter her class?

15. NIGEL PERKINS

Last week, Nigel Perkins flew to Monte Carlo with his wife to visit their son, Ronny. Nigel and his wife go to Monte Carlo two or three times every year between November and March because Ronny is too busy the other half of the year to be with them. They drove to Gatwick Airport on Wednesday morning and left the car at the airport parking lot. They had first class reservations for the two-hour flight. The plane left Gatwick on time at 11:15 and got to Monte Carlo ten minutes early, at five minutes past one. Nigel and his wife weren't expecting to meet Ronny at the airport, so they caught a taxi and went to his apartment near the port. They were surprised to find that their son wasn't at home. Nigel didn't have a key to theapartment, so he and his wife spent some time looking at the shop windows along the street. After 20 minutes, they went back to the apartment building and tried again. Ronny still wasn't there. The temperature was around 15 degrees and Nigel's wife felt a little cold. They decided to go to a small bookshop about 300 meters from Ronny's apartment building. Nigel likes to spend time in bookshops, but his wife, Margaret, doesn't, so Nigel asked permission to use the telephone and called Ronny's mobile number. Ronny was in a meeting with a tour operator not far from the bookshop. He said he was sorry and told Nigel that the porter in his apartment building had a key to his apartment. Nigel and Margaret walked back to the building, called the porter, and asked for the key. Ronny arrived two hours later.

15. NIGEL PERKINS

1. Where city did Nigel fly to last week?
2. Who did he go with?
3. Who did they go to Monte Carlo to visit?
4. How often do they fly to Monte Carlo?
5. In what period of the year do they go there?
6. Why don't they go there in the summer?
7. What airport did they leave from?
8. Did they drive to the airport or take a taxi?
9. What day did they fly to Monte Carlo?
10. Where did they leave their car?
11. What kind of reservations did they have on the flight?
12. Did the plane leave late or on time?
13. What time did it leave?
14. Did it get to Monte Carlo early or late?
15. What time did the flight arrive?
16. Who met them at the airport?
17. Were they expecting to meet Ronny at the airport?
18. Did they catch a bus or a taxi?
19. Did they go to Ronny's office or to his apartment?
20. Where is the apartment?
21. Was Ronny at home when they got there?
22. What was their reaction to this?
23. Did they go up to the apartment?
24. Why didn't they go up to the apartment?
25. What did they do?
26. How much time did they spend looking at the shops?
27. What did they do then?
28. Was Ronny there the second time?
29. How was the weather that day in Monte Carlo?
30. What was Margaret's problem?
31. Where did they decide to go?
32. How far was the bookshop from Ronny's apartment?
33. How do Nigel and Margaret feel about bookshops?
34. What did Nigel ask permission to do in the bookshop?
35. What telephone number did he call?
36. Where was Ronny?
37. Who was he in a meeting with?
38. What did he tell Nigel concerning the porter?
39. What did Nigel and his wife do after talking to Ronny?
40. When did Ronny get home?

16. NATASHA ZARAKOVICH

Last night Natasha had a big surprise. Yesterday was her birthday and she thought that nobody at the laboratory knew. She didn't want to tell them because Russian people always bring a lot of food to the office to celebrate and Natasha was on a strict diet. But she didn't remember that her boss, Gregori, was going out a lot with one of her best friends, Karina. Gregori and Karina had lunch together yesterday and Karina told him that it was Natasha's birthday. At 4:20, ten minutes before Natasha was planning to go to the national library, as she does every day, Gregori called her on the phone and asked her to help him with a report he was trying to get finished before 5:30. She thought this was strange, because Gregori doesn't usually ask her to work late. At 4:30, she went to his office on the third floor. When she got there, there were 10 people with cakes and tea waiting to celebrate her birthday. They stayed in the office, having a good time, until 7:00 p.m. Then Gregori invited all of them to a nightclub in the center of Moscow where there was good vodka and a gypsy group that played folk music. They stayed at the nightclub, eating, drinking and dancing until 10:30. Natasha got home at 11:00. She talked to her mother for a few minutes and then went to bed, because she had to get up early this morning to go to the laboratory. She was glad that today was Friday.

16. NATASHA ZARAKOVICH

1. What kind of surprise did Natasha have last night?
2. What was special for Natasha yesterday?
3. What did she think concerning the people at the lab?
4. Did she want to tell them about her birthday?
5. Why didn't she want to tell them?
6. Why didn't she want to eat a lot of food?
7. What didn't she remember about her boss, Gregori?
8. What did Gregori and Karina do yesterday?
9. What did Karina tell him?
10. What time was Natasha planning to go to the library?
11. What time did Gregori call her?
12. What did he ask her to help him with?
13. When did he say he wanted to finish the report?
14. Did Natasha think this was normal or strange?
15. Why did she think this was strange?
16. Where did she go at 4:30?
17. Where is Gregori's office?
18. How many people were there when she got there?
19. Were they waiting for her or for Gregori?
20. What did they want to celebrate?
21. What did they have waiting for her?
22. How long did they stay in the office?
23. Did they have a good time?
24. Where did Gregori invite them?
25. Where was the nightclub?
26. Was there good vodka or good brandy at the club?
27. What kind of music did the gypsy group play?
28. What did they do at the nightclub?
29. What time did they leave the night-club?
30. What time did Natasha get home?
31. What did she do before she went to bed?
32. How long did she talk to her mother?
33. Did she have to get up early or late this morning?
34. What was she glad about this morning?

17. AKI MORITA

Last Friday, Aki Morita had a meeting with his boss and with his boss's boss. He knew he was going to have the meeting but he thought that the subject of the meeting was going to be about a new supplier. However, when he got to the meeting room, Aki's boss offered him a coffee and told him that the meeting was about Louisiana. At first, Aki didn't understand. Then he remembered that Honda was building a new factory in the United States, in a city called Baton Rouge. He didn't know why his bosses wanted to talk about the new factory in Louisiana, but he tried to be calm. His direct boss told him that Honda wanted a good man to go to Louisiana to organize the quality department. He told Aki that it was necessary to establish the same quality system in the United States that, thanks to Aki, was so successful in Japan. Aki didn't know what to say. He immediately thought about his family. He asked his boss about the duration of the stay in Louisiana and his boss told him that it was for three years or maybe more. Aki speaks English well but his wife doesn't. His two children are young and they have English classes every day at school. He told his bosses that he wanted to discuss the matter with his family. They said that they needed an answer by next week. Aki went home after the meeting. He got home at 9:30. His wife was busy helping the children with their homework. Aki decided to tell her about the offer... or order... to go to the United States, the next day, which was Saturday.

17. AKI MORITA

1. When did Aki have the meeting?
2. How many other people were there in the meeting?
3. Who did Aki have the meeting with?
4. Did he know about the meeting in advance?
5. Did he think he knew the subject of the meeting?
6. What did he think the subject was going to be?
7. Was the meeting in an office or in a meeting room?
8. When he got there, what did his boss offer him?
9. What did his boss say the meeting was about?
10. What was Aki's first reaction?
11. What did he remember?
12. Where was the factory going to be exactly?
13. Was Aki nervous?
14. Did he understand the reason for the meeting at first?
15. What did his boss tell him that Honda needed?
16. What kind of department did they want to organize?
17. Did they want to establish the same quality system?
18. Was the system successful in Japan?
19. Who did Aki immediately think about?
20. What did he ask his boss about?
21. How long will the stay in Louisiana be?
22. What can you say about Aki's English?
23. What can you say about his wife's English?
24. What can you say about the age of his children?
25. What kind of classes do they have every day?
26. Do they take the classes at home?
27. Where do they take their English classes?
28. Did Aki accept the offer during the meeting?
29. What did he tell his bosses?
30. When did they say they needed an answer?
31. Did Aki visit a supplier after the meeting?
32. What did he do after the meeting?
33. What time did he get home?
34. Was his wife at home when he got there?
35. What was she doing when he got there?
36. Did Aki tell her about the meeting?
37. When did he decide to tell her?
38. Did he consider the situation an offer or an order?
39. Was the next day Tuesday?
40. What day was the next day?

18. PIERRE MONET

Pierre Monet considers himself an artist and a technician in the difficult job of translating. He was happy because he was going to meet the Prime Minister of France the next day. The Prime Minister wanted to congratulate Pierre on a job well done. For Pierre, it was simply another translation job and he did it like he did every translation. This time, however, he had done a special job. Last Tuesday, he received a document from the office of the Prime Minister. It was a speech in French that the Prime Minister was going to give in front of the British Parliament in English. The instructions were simply to translate the document into English. However, Pierre knew that the Prime Minister didn't speak English well, so he made the decision to translate the speech into simple, direct English. The problem was that the Prime Minister always wrote his speeches in complicated French, so Pierre had to do more than translate; he had to change the style of the speech completely without changing the power of the message. He started on the document at 9:30 in the morning and finished it just before 3:00 p.m. His boss sent the translation by special e-mail to the office of the Prime Minister. Two days later, the boss received a telephone call from the Prime Minister himself, inviting him and Pierre to a coffee the next day. The Prime Minister told Pierre's boss that when he read the speech, he was surprised at first. It was so different from the speech in French. But as he continued reading it, he saw that the message was perfectly expressed. In fact, he thought that Pierre's version was a new speech that was more effective and more powerful than the original. Pierre's boss congratulated him. He was as excited as his translator about the opportunity to have a coffee with the Prime Minister.

18. PIERRE MONET

1. How does Pierre consider himself?
2. Does he consider translating a difficult job?
3. Who was he going to meet the next day?
4. Who did the Prime Minister want to congratulate?
5. What did he want to congratulate him for?
6. How did Pierre consider this translation?
7. Did he do a special job this time or a normal job?
8. When did he receive the document?
9. Was it a speech or a report?
10. Was it in French or in English?
11. Who was the Prime Minister going to speak to?
12. What language was he going to use in the speech?
13. Were the translation instructions simple or difficult?
14. What did Pierre know about the Prime Minister?
15. What decision did he make?
16. What can you say about the Prime Minister's style?
17. What did Pierre decide to change in the speech?
18. What did he have to maintain in the speech?
19. What time did he start on the translation?
20. What time did he finish?
21. Who sent the translation to the Prime Minister?
22. How did he send it?
23. Who did his boss receive a phone call from?
24. How many days later did he receive it?
25. Who did the Prime Minister invite to his office?
26. What did he invite them to?
27. Did he invite them for the next day or for later?
28. Did the Prime Minister read the speech?
29. Was he surprised or angry at first?
30. Did he continue reading the speech?
31. What was his opinion about the message?
32. What did he think about Pierre's version?
33. Who did Pierre's boss congratulate?
34. Why was he excited?

19. DENISE JOHNSON

Last Monday, Denise Johnson was nervous. She was in her ballet class after school and the teacher told her and the other students that a woman was coming to give them an examination on Thursday. The woman was from the American Academy of Dance. The exam was held every year for all the girls who wanted to continue with ballet under the supervision of the Academy. If they passed this first exam, then they became members of the Academy and started officially in the category of elementary one. The teacher told the students to go home and tell their parents that the exam cost 15 dollars and the membership 10 dollars a year. Denise didn't like to take examinations. She always got very nervous when she had to take a test or an exam. That night, she told her mother about the exam and the Academy. She also told her that she didn't want to become a member because she didn't like to take exams. Nancy told Denise that the teacher thought she had a lot of potential. She told her that she had good technique and that the exam was probably very easy. Denise still didn't want to take the exam. The next day, after school, Nancy took her daughter to the best shop in Lincoln for ballet shoes. They bought a pair of beautiful shoes and other things. Denise liked the shoes so much that she decided to take the exam. Nancy knew that Denise only needed a little persuasion in a special way.

19. DENISE JOHNSON

1. When was Denise nervous?
2. Where was she when she became nervous?
3. Was the class before or after school?
4. Was she alone or was she with the other students?
5. Who did the teacher tell them was coming?
6. Where was this woman from?
7. What was she going to give the students?
8. When was she going to give the exam?
9. How often was the exam held?
10. Did all the girls have to take the exam?
11. Which girls had to take the exam?
12. Was this the first or the second exam?
13. What did they become if they passed the exam?
14. What category did they start in?
15. What did the teacher tell them to tell their parents?
16. Did Denise want to take the exam?
17. Why didn't she want to take it?
18. When did she tell her mother about the exam?
19. Did she want to become a member of the Academy?
20. Why didn't she want to become a member?
21. What did the teacher think about Denise's potential?
22. Did Nancy tell her she had good technique or style?
23. Did she tell her that the exam was easy or difficult?
24. Did this convince Denise to take the exam?
25. Where did Nancy take Denise?
26. When did she take her to the shop?
27. What did they buy?
28. What was Denise's opinion of the ballet shoes?
29. What did she decide to do?
30. What did Nancy know about her daughter?

20. LUIGI BARGHINI

Luigi Barghini spent three days in Germany last week. He flew to Stuttgart with his daughter, Anna, the General Manager of Luigi's company. They stayed at the Regency Hotel. On the first day, they had a meeting in the morning with the Chairman of Mercedes Benz. The meeting started at 11:00 a.m. and lasted 45 minutes. They spent a lot of the 45 minutes talking about the Agnelli family at Fiat. At 12 o'clock, Luigi and Anna had lunch with the Chairman and with the Managing Director in the private dining room on the top floor. They talked about the market situation for luxury cars and about the competition from Japanese car makers. After lunch, Luigi and Anna went back to the hotel and spent two hours planning the three meetings for the next day. In the evening, they had dinner with the Purchasing Manager of Mercedes, Karl Polster. Karl knew Anna very well because the two companies were negotiating a contract for car seats. Karl was 34 years old and single and he liked Anna very much. He was in favor of working with Luigi's company because he wanted to continue seeing Anna as much as possible. She was beautiful and rich. He knew that she was single but he didn't know if she was having a relationship with anyone in Italy. During dinner, Luigi noticed that Karl was paying a lot of attention to Anna, but he didn't say anything to his daughter later that night. He wanted to concentrate on the important meetings for the next day.

20. LUIGI BARGHINI

1. When did Luigi Barghini go to Germany?
2. How many days did he stay there?
3. What city did he fly to?
4. Did he go to Stuttgart alone?
5. Who did he fly to Stuttgart with?
6. What hotel did they stay at?
7. Did they have three meetings on the first day?
8. How many meetings did they have on the first day?
9. Who did they have the meeting with?
10. Did they talk about a possible contract?
11. What family did they talk about during the meeting?
12. Who did Luigi and Anna have lunch with?
13. Did they have lunch in a local restaurant?
14. Where did they have lunch?
15. What two things did they talk about during lunch?
16. Did Luigi and Anna stay at Mercedes after lunch?
17. Where did they go after lunch?
18. What did they spend two hours doing?
19. How many meetings did they have for the next day?
20. Who did they have dinner with in the evening?
21. Did Karl know Anna?
22. Why did he know her?
23. How old was Karl?
24. Was he married or single?
25. Why did he want to work with Luigi's company?
26. Why was he interested in Anna?
27. What didn't he know about Anna's life in Italy?
28. What did Luigi notice about Karl during dinner?
29. Did he say anything to her about Karl's attention?
30. Why didn't he say anything to her?

21. LI TONG

Yesterday, Li Tong decided to learn English. He made the decision at exactly 11:15 in the morning. He was working in the telephone factory, as usual. At about 11:00, Li saw one of the young employees from the process engineering department with two tall men who appeared to be English or American. They were wearing ties. The young employee was talking to them in English and explaining the production process. At one moment, the young employee asked Li a few questions about his job. Li explained that he was responsible for inserting the microphone in the telephone receiver. Then the young employee said two or three sentences to the foreign men and they looked at the work that Li was doing. They smiled at Li and said something in English. He supposed they said "thank you" and he said "thank you" in Chinese. Then the three people left and continued walking around the factory. Li went back to his work, but he was thinking about the young Chinese employee. Li was sure that the young man probably earned a lot more money than him. He knew that the company was growing very fast. Some of the workers in the factory were now in office jobs and were earning more money than he did. At that moment, he made the decision to learn English. He didn't know how much it cost to take classes, but he decided to ask one of his friends who was working in the same department as the young man. He knew that his friend was going to a language school less than 500 meters from where Li lived.

21. LI TONG

1. What did Li Tong decide to do yesterday?
2. When did he make the decision?
3. Where was he working at that moment?
4. Did he see a young man or an old man at 11:00?
5. Was the young man Chinese or American?
6. Was the young man with two men or with three?
7. Were the men tall or short?
8. What did Li see that the two men were wearing?
9. Did they appear to be Japanese?
10. What nationality did they appear to be?
11. What language was the young man speaking?
12. What process was he explaining to the two men?
13. What kind of questions did the young man ask Li?
14. What did Li tell him that he was responsible for?
15. Did the young employee translate what Li said?
16. What did the two foreigners do concerning Li's work?

17. Did they say something to Li?
18. What language did they speak to him in?
19. Did Li answer them in English or in Chinese?
20. What did Li think they said to him?
21. What did he say to them?
22. What did the three men do after saying "thank you"?
23. Did Li take a break or go back to his work?
24. Which of the three people did he think about?
25. What was he sure about concerning the young man?
26. What did Li know about the company?
27. Where were some ex-factory workers working now?
28. Were they earning more or less than Li?
29. What did Li decide to do at that moment?
30. What didn't he know about taking English classes?
31. Who did he decide to ask?
32. What department did his friend work in?
33. What did Li know about his friend?
34. Where was the language school?

22. INÉS GARCÍA

Yesterday, Inés García had a traffic accident. It happened at about 5:45 p.m. when she was driving to the University of Seville for her evening course in Business Management and Finance. The accident was her fault. She was driving her car, a Ford Puma, through the narrow streets in the center of Seville. At the same time, she was talking with Paco, her boyfriend, on her mobile telephone. She was listening to her boyfriend and didn't notice a stop sign in front of her. She ran the stop sign and another car hit her on the passenger side. Fortunately, it was a small car too, an Opel Corsa, and, as a result, the accident wasn't serious. Inés cut her phone conversation and got out of the car. She went to the other car to speak to the driver. She was happy to see that the other driver was a young man, probably the same age as Inés. When he got out of his car, he smiled and said hello in Spanish but with a French accent. Inés simply looked at him and didn't say anything. He was tall and very attractive. He seemed like a very pleasant person. Inés usually talks a lot, but this time she didn't know what to say. The young man asked her if she had her car papers. Inés went back to her car and got the papers. They finished the paperwork in less than ten minutes. Then, the young Frenchman, whose name was François Monet, invited her to have a coffee in a coffee shop across the street. Inés accepted and disconnected her mobile telephone.

22. INÉS GARCÍA

1. What happened to Inés yesterday?
2. Did it happen in the morning?
3. When did it happen?
4. Where was she going at the time?
5. Why was she going to the University?
6. Whose fault was the accident?
7. What kind of car was she driving?
8. What part of Seville was she driving through?
9. What can you say about the streets in that area?
10. What was she doing while she was driving?
11. Who was she talking to?
12. What didn't she notice in front of her?
13. Did she run the stop sign or did she stop in time?
14. Did she hit another car or did another car hit her?
15. Where did the other car hit her?
16. Was the other car big or small?
17. What kind of car was it?
18. What can you say about the accident?
19. Why wasn't the accident serious?
20. What did Inés do regarding her phone conversation?
21. Did she get out of her car or stay in it?
22. Did she go to the other car or stay next to hers?
23. Why did she go to the other car?
24. Why was she happy when she saw the other driver?
25. How old was the other driver?
26. Did the other driver smile when he got out of his car?
27. What did he say to Inés when he got out of his car?
28. Did he say hello in Spanish or in French?
29. What kind of accent did he have?
30. What did Inés do when the man said hello to her?
31. Describe the man physically.
32. Did he seem like a pleasant or unpleasant person?
33. Does Inés usually talk a lot or very little?
34. Did she talk a lot this time too?
35. Why didn't she talk a lot?
36. What did the young man ask her?
37. Did Inés go back to her car or call her boyfriend?
38. What did she get from her car?
39. How long did it take them to finish the paperwork?
40. What was the young Frenchman's name?
41. What did he invite her to have with him?
42. Where was the coffee shop?
43. Did Inés accept or reject the invitation?
44. What did she do concerning her mobile telephone?

23. MICHAEL JOHNSON

Last Saturday, Michael Johnson was the star of his basketball team. They were playing in the regional finals. His team won the game easily. The final score was 67 to 42. The other team was the favorite to win the game, but Michael set a team record and a record for the state of Nebraska. He scored 41 points during the game, 16 points in the first half and 25 points in the second half. The next day his picture was in the Lincoln newspaper, with a long article about the game. Michael made seven baskets in the first three minutes of the second half and only two of his points during the game were free throws. The next day, after Michael read the article, he started to receive phone calls from some of his friends. He also received a phone call from the basketball coach at the high school that he was going to attend next year. The coach told Michael that he was going to watch the next game between Michael's school and the Omaha Buffaloes. The coach told Michael that the Buffaloes were the best basketball team in Nebraska at middle school level. Michael wasn't worried. He knew that the Buffaloes were not a good defensive team. Michael planned to play the same way as in the last game. He was sure that with a little luck his team was going to win. His father agreed with him, but his mother told him that he needed to concentrate more on his studies and less on basketball.

23. MICHAEL JOHNSON

1. What was Michael last Saturday?
2. Were they playing in the state or regional finals?
3. Did his team win easily or with difficulty?
4. What was the final score?
5. Which team was the favorite to win the game?
6. Did Michael set one or two records?
7. What two records did Michael set?
8. Did he score more or less than 30 points?
9. How many points did he score?
10. Did he score more points in the first or second half?
11. How many points did he score in the first half?
12. How many points did he score in the second half?
13. Was there a press photographer at the game?
14. What was in the Lincoln newspaper the next day?
15. What happened at the beginning of the second half?
16. How many of his points were free throws?
17. Did Michael read the article in the newspaper?
18. What did he start to receive from his friends?
19. Did he receive a call from a basketball coach?
20. Where was the basketball coach from?
21. What game was the coach going to watch?
22. Was the next game against another Lincoln school?
23. What team was the next game against?
24. What did the coach tell Michael about the Buffaloes?
25. Was Michael worried about the Buffaloes?
26. What did he know about the Buffaloes?
27. How did he plan to play the game against them?
28. What was he sure about?
29. What was his father's opinion about this?
30. What did his mother tell him that he needed to do?

24. PAULA EISENBACH

Last Tuesday, Paula Eisenbach spent the afternoon with Tom Sanders. She spent about 10 hours a week helping him with drawings for the Disney Corporation. Tom was a student at the University of Heidelberg like Paula, but he also had a contract with Disney to draw cartoons for Disney animated movies. Tom was an excellent artist and Paula liked working with him because she learned a lot about drawing technique. Tom paid her $15 an hour for her work. He paid her in dollars because the Disney Corporation paid him in dollars too. During their drawing session, Tom told Paula that he wanted to take her to California to meet his parents. Paula knew that Tom wanted to take her to California, but she wasn't sure that she wanted to go. She liked Tom as a person, but she wasn't sure about her feelings for him. He was a wonderful person and a fantastic artist, but Paula felt she wasn't ready to expand her relationship with him. She didn't understand his reason for inviting her to California because they were only friends. That night, she called her parents in Munich and told them about the situation with Tom. Her father told her that she had to make the decision herself. Her mother told her that it wasn't a good idea. She said that if Paula didn't feel anything special for Tom now, then it was dangerous for her to go to California with him. Paula decided to think about it for a few days before giving Tom a final answer.

24. PAULA EISENBACH

1. Who did Paula spend last Tuesday with?
2. Did she spend the morning or afternoon with him?
3. How many hours a week did she work with him?
4. Did she help him with his studies?
5. What did she help him with?
6. Did Tom work with Disney or Warner Brothers?
7. What kind of contract did Tom have with Disney?
8. What did Paula think about Tom as an artist?
9. Did she like working with him?
10. Why did she like working with him?
11. How much did Tom pay her for her work?
12. Did he pay her in dollars or in euros?
13. Why did he pay her in dollars?
14. What did Tom tell Paula during the drawing session?
15. Was this a surprise for Paula?
16. Did she know that he wanted her to go with him?
17. Did she want to go?
18. Did she like Tom?
19. What wasn't she sure about concerning Tom?
20. What kind of person did she consider Tom?
21. What did she feel that she wasn't ready to do?
22. What didn't she understand about the invitation?
23. What was the relationship between Paula and Tom?
24. Who did Paula call that night?
25. Where did her parents live?
26. What situation did she tell them about?
27. What did her father tell her?
28. What did her mother tell her?
29. What did her mother say was dangerous?
30. What did Paula decide to do?

25. NIGEL PERKINS

This week has been a busy one for Nigel. He's had to work more than usual because his company has discovered some very important evidence. Two months ago, a large life insurance company asked Nigel's firm to investigate an unusual case. A 62 year-old man had died six months before and his 32 year-old wife, an ex-model, had received seven million dollars from the insurance company. The man died of a heart attack. During the investigation, Nigel's company discovered that the woman had bought a large amount of medicine for people who suffer hemophilia. It is the worst kind of medicine for people who have bad blood circulation. Nigel was a good friend of the man who had died. He felt that it was his obligation to help personally in the investigation.

25. NIGEL PERKINS

1. Has this been an easy week for Nigel?
2. What kind of week has this one been for him?
3. Has he had to work more or less than usual?
4. What has his company discovered?
5. What kind of company contacted Nigel's firm?
6. How long ago did they contact his firm?
7. What did they want Nigel's firm to investigate?
8. How old was the man who had died 6 months before?
9. Was he married or single when he died?
10. Was his wife the same age as him?
11. How old was she when her husband died?
12. What was her profession before getting married?
13. How much money did she receive when he died?
14. Who did she receive the money from?
15. How did her husband die?
16. Did Nigel's company investigate his death?
17. Did the insurance company suspect something?
18. Did Nigel's company find anything suspicious?
19. What did they discover that the woman had bought?
20. Did she buy a large or small amount of this medicine?
21. What people usually buy this medicine?
22. This medicine is the worst kind for what kind of people?
23. Did the woman's husband suffer from hemophilia?
24. Did the man probably have a circulation problem?
25. Did Nigel know the man personally?
26. What was his relationship with the man?
27. Did Nigel help personally in the investigation?
28. Why did he help personally?

26. INÉS GARCÍA

Inés García has had a difficult day today. She's attended two meetings with her colleagues in the law firm, she's gone to the courthouse twice to defend two different labor cases and she's given a lecture on labor law to firstyear law students at the University of Seville. She's had to do all these things in a period of 8 hours. Because of this, she hasn't had time to do three other things that need her attention. She hasn't had time today to buy a birthday present for her boyfriend, whose birthday is the day after tomorrow. She hasn't had time either to make an appointment with the dentist to repair a crown that broke yesterday. Finally, she hasn't had time to do the most important thing, which is to talk to François Monet, the young man from Paris whom she met in the car accident two weeks ago. He left a message on her mobile phone this morning while she was in one of the meetings in the law firm. She's tried to call him three times today, but his line has been busy all day. She's spoken to him twice since the accident and he's invited her to Paris. She spent three days in Paris with her parents when she was 11 years old, but since then, she hasn't had the opportunity to go back. She's been thinking a lot about François in the last two weeks and she's made the decision to start learning French. She hasn't told her boyfriend anything yet.

26. INÉS GARCÍA

1. Has Inés had an easy day today?
2. What kind of day has she had?
3. Has she attended three meetings today?
4. How many meetings has she attended?
5. Has she gone to the courthouse today?
6. How many times has she been there?
7. How many different cases has she defended today?
8. What kind of cases has she defended?
9. What else has she done today?
10. In how much time has she done all these things?
11. How many things hasn't she had time to do?
12. What hasn't she done yet concerning her boyfriend?
13. When's his birthday?
14. What hasn't she done concerning her dentist?
15. Does she need to go to the dentist?
16. Why does she need to go to the dentist?
17. What's the most important thing she hasn't done?
18. Who is François Monet?
19. When was the car accident?
20. What did François leave on Inés' mobile phone?
21. Why didn't Inés answer her phone when he called?
22. How many times has she tried to return the call?
23. Why hasn't she been able to talk to him?
24. How long has his line been busy?
25. Has she spoken to him since the accident?
26. How many times has she spoken to him?
27. Has he invited her to Paris?
28. Has Inés ever been to Paris?
29. When did she go to Paris?
30. How many days did she spend there?
31. How many times has she been back since then?
32. Who has Inés been thinking a lot about lately?
33. What decision has she made?
34. Who hasn't she told about François?

27. NATASHA ZARAKOVICH

Natasha has been thinking about Scotland for the past two weeks. Her cousin, André Zarakovich, has been living in Scotland for 23 years. He moved there with his parents when he was only five years old. He is one year younger than Natasha. Many years ago, when André was a child, he played with Natasha every day in Moscow. They lived next door to each other. André only remembers a few things from that period. However, Natasha still remembers a lot of things. She remembers that André was a bad little boy. He always hit her when they were playing. For the past five years, André and Natasha have been writing to each other. André's father is an aeronautical engineer and the family has a nice house in the suburbs of Glasgow. Ever since André started writing to Natasha, he has been inviting her to visit him and his family in Glasgow. Natasha would like to go, but it's too expensive for her. In his last letter, André told her that he had found a new job and that he was earning twice as much as in his last job. He also told her that, with the extra money in the first two months, he had made a flight reservation for Natasha on British Airways for December 22nd. The return ticket was for January 3rd. When Natasha read the letter, she couldn't believe it. She didn't like the idea of André paying for the ticket, but she was excited that she was finally going to visit another country. She's never been outside of Russia. In fact, she's never been more than 50 kilometers outside of Moscow.

27. NATASHA ZARAKOVICH

---

1. What has Natasha been thinking about lately?

2. How long has she been thinking about Scotland?

3. What's her cousin's name?

4. How long has he been living in Scotland?

5. Did he move there alone or with his parents?

6. How old was he when he moved to Scotland?

7. How much younger is he than Natasha?

8. Where did André live when he was a young child?

9. Did he live near Natasha or far from her?

10. What did they do together at that time?

11. How much does André remember from that period?

12. How much does Natasha remember?

13. What kind of boy was André when he was little?

14. What did he do to Natasha when they were together?

15. How long have they been writing to each other?

16. What does André's father do?

17. What kind of house does André's family have?

18. Where do they live in Glasgow?

19. Since when has André been inviting Natasha to Scotland?

20. Would Natasha like to go?

21. What's the problem?

22. What did André tell Natasha about his working life?

23. How much more does he earn in his new job?

24. What did he do with the extra money he is earning?

25. With what airline did he make a reservation?

26. When will Natasha go to Scotland?

27. Will she stay in Scotland for several months?

28. When will she go back to Moscow?

29. What was Natasha's reaction when she read the letter?

30. What didn't she like about the arrangement?

31. Why was she excited?

32. How many times has she traveled abroad?

33. How many times has she been to St.Petersburg?

34. Has she ever been to another large city in Russia?

35. Has she ever been outside of Moscow?

36. How far outside of Moscow has she been?

28. ANNA BARGHINI

This morning, shortly before lunch, Anna Barghini received a telephone call from Karl Polster, the Purchasing Manager of Mercedes Benz. They have been in contact for several months because Anna's company is negotiating a large contract to supply car seats for several models produced by Mercedes. Anna's having lunch right now in her office. She's thinking about Karl Polster. It seems strange that the Purchasing Manager of Mercedes should call her so often. His job is more administrative than technical. The real negotiations are between her engineers and the technical people at Mercedes. She has a feeling that Karl is interested in something more than business. In their conversation this morning, he asked her twice when she was planning to visit Stuttgart again. He also talked to her about a country house he has in the Black Forest. Anna doesn't have a serious relationship with any man right now. She's really too busy running her father's company to worry about men. However, she's 27 years old and she sometimes feels a little lonely. Karl is a nice young man and quite handsome, but Anna is always afraid that men are more interested in her money than in her. Her family's estate is worth over 50 million dollars. She told Karl in their conversation that she was planning to be in Stuttgart for a couple of days at the end of November. She didn't say anything when he mentioned his country house.

28. ANNA BARGHINI

1. Who did Anna receive a telephone call from?
2. When did she receive the call?
3. What's Karl's job at Mercedes Benz?
4. How long have they been in contact?
5. Why have they been in contact?
6. Is Anna having lunch or dinner right now?
7. Who is she thinking about?
8. What seems strange to Anna about Karl?
9. Is Karl's job more technical or more administrative?
10. Are the negotiations more technical or administrative?
11. Who are Anna's engineers dealing with at Mercedes?
12. What does Anna think Karl is interested in?
13. What did Karl ask Anna twice about this morning?
14. What else did he talk to her about?
15. What's Anna's situation now concerning men?
16. Why doesn't she have time for men right now?
17. How old is she?
18. How does she feel sometimes?
19. What is her opinion of Karl?
20. What is she afraid of concerning men?
21. How much is her family's estate worth?
22. Did she tell Karl that she was planning to be in Stuttgart?
23. When did she say she was planning to be there?
24. What did she say when Karl mentioned his country house?

29. AKI MORITA

Aki Morita was worried about his future in Honda. Earlier that day, his bosses had told him that he would be the quality manager at a new factory that Honda was building in Louisiana. That same night, before saying anything to his family, Aki looked up "Louisiana" in his encyclopedia. It said that Louisiana was famous for its French influence. A group of French Protestants called the "Acadians" had gone to Louisiana to escape persecution. They had established a special culture in Louisiana and they were called the "Cajuns", which was a deformation of the word "Acadians". The article also talked about the city of New Orleans and about the history of Louisiana. It said that there had been a lot of political corruption in the state during the '30's and '40's. The only thing that Aki found interesting was the section about the beautiful plantation homes along the Mississippi River, in a town called Natchez. He thought that his wife would enjoy visiting that town. When he had finished the article about Louisiana, he sat down to have dinner with his family. It was 8:30. His wife noticed that he was quiet during the meal, but she didn't say anything. She simply thought that he had had a hard day at the office. He was often quiet and pensive when he was at home.

29. AKI MORITA

1. What was Aki Morita worried about?
2. What had his bosses told him earlier the same day?
3. Did Aki tell his family about Louisiana when he got home?
4. What book did he get out when he got home?
5. What did he look up in the encyclopedia?
6. What did the article say Louisiana was famous for?
7. What group of people did the article talk about?
8. Why had they gone to Louisiana?
9. What was the name of the culture they had established?
10. Why was it called the "Cajun" culture?
11. What big city did the article mention?
12. Did Aki read about the history or the economy of Louisiana?
13. What did he read about the political situation in the '30's and '40's?
14. What did Aki find interesting in the article?
15. Where were the plantations located?
16. What did Aki think that his wife would enjoy?
17. What did he do after he had finished reading the article?
18. Who did he have dinner with?
19. What time did he sit down to have dinner?
20. What did his wife notice during the meal?
21. What did she say about this?
22. What did she think was the problem?
23. Was Aki usually fun and talkative when he was at home?
24. What was Aki usually like when he was at home?

Pierre Monet had a terrible time getting up this morning. If he hadn't had an important translation to do at the Ministry, he would've stayed in bed until at least 10 o'clock. But he had to get up at 6:30, his normal time to get up. The problem was that he had gone to bed at 4:00 a.m. He had spent ten hours doing an urgent translation for a personal client of his who needed the translation by 8 o'clock that very morning. When Pierre got home at 5:00 p.m. the day before, he began working on a relatively short, easy translation about a corporate merger.

30. PIERRE MONET

The translation needed to be done by the following Monday. At 5:30, however, he received a telephone call from the Chairman of Peugeot, who knew Pierre personally, and used his services for the translation of important documents. The Chairman told Pierre that a meeting that was scheduled for the following week with the management of Volvo in Sweden had been moved up to tomorrow. He said that he urgently needed Pierre to translate two letters and a 24-page contract. Pierre knew that this would mean staying up all night, but he told the Chairman not to worry. Within five minutes, Pierre received the letters and contract by e-mail and began translating. By 7:00 p.m., he had finished the two letters, one of which was four pages long. At 9:00 p.m., his wife made him a sandwich and a strong coffee. By that time, he had already finished the first six pages of the contract. However, the second half of the contract was quite difficult to translate. It included a lot of legal terminology and very long sentences. One sentence was so long that it took Pierre almost a minute to find the subject and the verb. By 3:00 a.m., he had finished the contract and he spent the next hour checking it thoroughly. Shortly before 4:00 a.m., he sent it to Peugeot by e-mail. Then he went to bed exhausted. His only consolation was that he would earn almost 1,000 euros for the job. It was worth it.

30. PIERRE MONET

1. What problem did Pierre have this morning?
2. What did he have at the Ministry this morning?
3. How long would he have stayed in bed if he hadn't had an important translation at the Ministry?
4. What time had he gone to bed the night before?
5. How many hours had he spent doing an important translation at home?
6. Did he do the translation for a personal client or for a client of the Ministry?
7. When did this client need the translation?
8. Did Pierre know about this translation when he got home the day before?
9. Did he start doing this translation when he got home?
10. What translation did he start doing?
11. By what day did this translation?
12. Who did he receive a phone call from need to be finished?
13. What time did he receive the call?
14. Did the Chairman of Peugeot know Pierre personally?
15. Why did he know him?
16. Who did the Chairman have a meeting with?
17. Where is Volvo located?
18. When was the meeting originally scheduled?
19. What had happened concerning the meeting?
20. What did the Chairman urgently need Pierre to do?
21. What would this mean for Pierre?
22. What did he tell the Chairman of Peugeot?
23. How soon did he receive the documents?
24. How did he receive them?
25. How far had he progressed by 7:00 p.m.?
26. How long was one of the letters?
27. What did his wife do at 9:00 p.m.?
28. How much had he already translated by that time?
29. What was the problem with the second half of the contract?
30. What did the second half of the contract include?
31. What problem did Pierre have with one sentence?
32. How far had he progressed by 3:00 a.m.?
33. What did he do between 3:00 and 4:00 a.m.?
34. When did he send the translation to Peugeot?
35. How did he send it to them?
36. How did he feel when he went to bed?
37. What was his only consolation?
38. What was his feeling about the effort he had made?

31. FRANÇOIS MONET

François Monet is Pierre's nephew. He's 27 years old and works in a large French chemical company. He's a salesman and he travels to many factories throughout the European Union. He often travels to Huelva, a small city not far from Seville, in Spain. When he goes to Seville, he always rents a car to drive to Huelva. That's how he met Inés García. They met because of a traffic accident. François thinks he was lucky to have the accident, because otherwise he wouldn't have met Inés. Now he thinks about her every day and calls her as often as he can. He's even invited her to visit Paris. However, he's a little afraid of having a more serious relationship with her because he doesn't understand the character of the people from the south of Spain, especially from Seville. They seem like fun people who look for ways to enjoy life. But he still remembers the opera he saw several years ago called "Carmen". In the opera, a young soldier fell in love with a gypsy girl from Seville. The poor soldier had all kinds of problems. Inés wasn't a gypsy girl, but sometimes she talked and behaved like the singer who played the role of Carmen in the opera. Inés had black hair and dark eyes. François found her very attractive and very different from the girls in Paris. The last time he spoke to her, he invited her to visit Paris. Since then, he's called her three times, but her mobile phone was disconnected each time. He hopes she'll call him.

31. FRANÇOIS MONET

1. How is François Monet related to Pierre Monet?
2. How old is he?
3. Does he work in a Spanish company?
4. Where does he work?
5. What's his job in the company?
6. Where does he travel in his job?
7. Where does he go when he travels to Spain?
8. How does he travel when he's in Spain?
9. How did he meet Inés García?
10. Why is he glad he had the accident?
11. How often does he think about Inés?
12. How often does he call her?
13. What has he invited her to do?
14. What is his feeling about having a serious relationship with her?
15. Why is he afraid?
16. What do the people from Seville seem like to him?

17. What opera did he see several years ago?
18. Who did the French soldier fall in love with?
19. What happened in his relationship with her?
20. Is Inés a gypsy?
21. What does François remember about the singer in the opera "Carmen"?
22. What can you say about Inés' physical features?
23. Does François find her attractive or ugly?
24. What did François think about her as compared with the girls in Paris?
25. What did François do the last time he spoke to Inés?
26. How many times has he called her since then?
27. Why hasn't he been able to talk to her again?
28. What does he hope?

32. LI TONG

Li Tong has just finished his very first English class. He's on his way home now. The language academy where he's just taken his class is located about a kilometer from his house. It took Li about 10 minutes to get there on his bike. When he got to the academy, he was sent to room 11, where there were seven other students waiting for the teacher to arrive. Li sat at the back of the room next to a large window. Outside he could see a lot of people coming and going, most of them on bicycles. At that moment, the teacher came into the room carrying a lot of books. He put them on a small desk in front of the class and then wrote his name on the board. Li didn't know what the teacher was writing because he didn't know the English or Latin alphabet. It looked like strange symbols to him. Then the teacher turned to face the class and said something, pointing to himself. Li assumed that the teacher was saying his name. It sounded like he was saying "pita". Then the teacher pointed at different students and said something that Li didn't understand. The first student just looked at the teacher, without saying anything. The student behind the first one whispered something to him, after which the first student said his name, "Han". Then the teacher made the first student say some strange sounds finishing with the name "Han". Li felt a little nervous because he knew the teacher was going to ask him the same question. He listened carefully to the other students as they answered the teacher with the same strange sounds, followed by their names. When it was Li's turn, he repeated the sounds, finishing with "Li". The teacher seemed satisfied, said something strange again and went back to the blackboard. Li realized that he had just said his first sentence in English.

32. LI TONG

1. Has Li Tong just finished work?
2. What has he just finished?
3. Where is he going now?
4. How far is the English academy from Li's house?
5. How long did it take Li to get there?
6. How did he go there?
7. When he got there, where was he sent?
8. How many students were there in the room when Li got there?
9. What were they doing?
10. Did Li sit at the front or at the back of the room?
11. What did he sit next to?
12. What could he see through the window?
13. What means of transportation were most of the people using?
14. Who came into the room while Li was looking out the window?
15. What was he carrying with him?
16. Where did he put the books?
17. Where was the desk located?
18. What did the teacher do after putting the books on the desk?
19. Did Li understand what the teacher wrote on the blackboard?
20. Why not?
21. What did the teacher's name look like to Li?
22. Why did the teacher point to himself?
23. What did Li assume the teacher was saying?
24. What did the teacher's name sound like to Li?
25. Who did the teacher point at after that?
26. How did the first student react?
27. What did the student behind the first one do?
28. How did the first student respond after the other student whispered something to him?
29. What did the teacher make the first student do after he said "Han"?
30. How did Li feel when the teacher started asking questions?
31. Why did he feel nervous?
32. What did Li do as the different students answered the teacher?
33. What did Li do when it was his turn?
34. How did the teacher react after Li answered the question?
35. Where did the teacher go after Li answered the question?
36. What did Li realize at that moment?

33. LUIGI BARGHINI

Luigi Barghini's son, Roberto, has just finished his engineering degree at the University of Milan. Luigi is very proud of him because he graduated second in his class. It took him six years instead of the usual five to get his degree, because he specialized in two different fields of industrial engineering: organization and robotics. It's very rare for a student to specialize in two different fields. In fact, it's usually not permitted, but four years ago, Roberto asked his father to speak to the Dean of the Engineering School at the university to get permission. Luigi thought that his son was a little crazy to want to study two different areas of engineering, but he helped his son get permission to do what he wanted. The Dean of the Engineering School knew Luigi quite well. Thirty years before, he had been one year ahead of him at the same university. They hadn't been close friends at that time, but since then, Luigi had asked his old school mate to send him the best young engineers graduating from the University of Milan. Thanks to some of these engineers, Luigi's company had become the second largest car seat manufacturer in Europe. Now Luigi has to make a decision about Roberto, who has just turned 24. Roberto would like to work as a consultant in organization and computer integrated systems. However, Luigi thinks he should work in the family company with his father and sister. Roberto has already received an offer to work for Accenture, a large American company with offices in Milan, and he is tempted to take the job. He thinks that his sister, Anna, is perfectly capable of running the family business with Luigi's help and, besides, he doesn't see much challenge in working in a car seat factory, even if it's the second biggest in Europe. Luigi thinks that, with Anna and Roberto, the company could easily become the number one supplier of car seats in Europe.

33. LUIGI BARGHINI

1. What has Roberto just finished?
2. Did he study engineering in the U.K.?
3. Where did he study engineering?
4. Why is Luigi proud of him?
5. How long did it take him to get his degree?
6. How long does it usually take to get a degree?
7. Why did it take Roberto one more year?
8. What fields of engineering did he specialize in?
9. Why is it rare for people to specialize in two fields?
10. What did Roberto ask his father to do four years ago?
11. What did Luigi think about Roberto's plans?
12. Did Luigi help his son get permission?
13. Why was Luigi able to get permission for his son?
14. Why did he know the Dean of Engineering?
15. How long ago did they study together?

16. Who is older, Luigi or the Dean?
17. Were they close friends when they were studying?
18. Why did Luigi stay in contact with the Dean?
19. What had these young engineers done for Luigi?
20. What kind of decision does Luigi have to make?
21. How old is Roberto?
22. What would he like to do for a living?
23. What does Luigi think he should do?
24. What company has Roberto received an offer from?
25. Where are the world headquarters of Accenture?
26. Where are the Italian offices?
27. What is Roberto tempted to do regarding Accenture?
28. What does he think about his sister, Anna?
29. What does he think about working in his father's company?
30. What does Luigi think Roberto and Anna can achieve if they work together?

34. PAULA EISENBACH

Paula Eisenbach feels relieved today. Yesterday, she told her friend Tom Sanders that she had decided not to go to California with him during the Christmas holidays. Tom was very upset and they had a long argument. Finally, Paula had to tell him the truth. She told him that she enjoyed working with him and that she had learned a lot. Then she told him that she wasn't ready to have a deeper relationship. Tom got angry and told her that he didn't want her to help him anymore with the Disney drawings. Paula knew he would react that way. She had been helping him for almost two months and she was becoming more and more convinced that Tom wasn't a stable person. He was a brilliant artist but he was very introverted. He didn't know how to respond to people in a natural way. Last night, Paula called her parents in Munich and told them her decision. Her mother was relieved and her father told her that she had made the right decision. They told her they were thinking about spending a week in the Canary Islands during the Christmas holidays and asked her if she would like to go. Paula jumped at the opportunity. She was tired of the cold weather in Heidelberg. A few days in the Canary Islands would be the perfect remedy.

34. PAULA EISENBACH

1. How does Paula Eisenbach feel today?
2. Who did she speak to yesterday?
3. What did she tell him that she had decided?
4. Was Tom relieved?
5. How did he react?
6. Did they discuss the matter calmly or did they argue?
7. What did Paula finally tell Tom?
8. What did she say exactly?
9. When Tom got angry, what did he tell her?
10. Was this a surprise for Paula? Why not?
11. How long had she been helping him?
12. What had she become convinced of?
13. What kind of artist was Tom in Paula's opinion?
14. Was he introverted or extroverted?
15. What, in Paula's opinion, was his problem regarding people?
16. Who did Paula call last night?
17. What did she tell them?
18. How did her mother react?
19. What did her father tell her?
20. What did they say they were thinking about doing?
21. What did they ask her?
22. How did Paula react to the invitation?
23. What was she tired of?
24. What was her feeling about spending a few days in the Canary Islands?

35. NANCY JOHNSON

Nancy Johnson has a problem. If she had problems like this one every day, she and her family would be rich by now. Her problem is that she's been offered a job to decorate the home that George Clooney owns in Aspen, Colorado, the most famous ski resort in the United States. It would mean spending at least one week out of every month in Aspen. This evening, she will discuss the problem with her husband, Phillip, and then call Eddie Campbell to let him know her final decision. Eddie is a famous interior decorator and the most prestigious professor of interior design in California. He teaches at U.C.L.A., which stands for the University of California at Los Angeles. He and his students often help the Hollywood rich to decorate their homes in Beverly Hills and Malibu Beach. He knows Nancy Johnson very well because they studied interior design together at the University of Kansas. Eddie and his students decorated George Clooney's home in Beverly Hills seven years ago. Last week, Mr. Clooney called Eddie, asking him to decorate his new home in Colorado. Since Eddie couldn't do it, he told Mr. Clooney that he had the perfect person for the job. Now Nancy has to make a decision. Her mother and sister live in Coffeyville, Kansas. Her sister is single. If they could come up to Lincoln from time to time to stay with the kids, then maybe Nancy could have time to go to Colorado and do the job. Also, she's sure that the technical school where she works would give her the time off as well. It would mean a lot for the school to have a teacher who's decorating the home of George Clooney. "What will Phillip say?" she thought.

35. NANCY JOHNSON

1. Does Nancy Johnson have a problem?
2. Is it a serious problem or a pleasant problem?
3. What would her economic status be like if she had problems like this one every day?
4. What job has she been offered?
5. Where is George Clooney's home?
6. What is Aspen, Colorado famous for?
7. Who will she discuss the problem with this evening?
8. Who will she call after making a final decision?
9. Who is Eddie Campbell?
10. Where does he teach interior design?
11. What does U.C.L.A. stand for?
12. Does Eddie only teach or does he do other things?
13. What other things does he do?
14. Who helps him?
15. Where do the Hollywood rich have their homes?
16. Does Eddie know Nancy well?
17. Why does he know her so well?
18. Where did they study together?
19. Why did George Clooney know Eddie personally?
20. When did Eddie and his students decorate his home?
21. When did Mr. Clooney call Eddie?
22. Why did he call him?
23. What did Eddie tell Mr. Clooney?
24. Who lives in Coffeyville, Kansas?
25. What is her sister's marital status?
26. What does Nancy think they could do?
27. If they came up to Lincoln, what could Nancy do?
28. How does she think the technical school will react?
29. Why does she think they'll say yes?
30. What is her only real doubt?

36. DENISE JOHNSON

Last Friday afternoon, Denise Johnson had a big fight with one of her best friends, Pamela Stanley. They were playing a guessing game in the backyard of another friend, Jenny, who lives on the same block as the other two. The rules of the game were simple. One person had to think of someone famous and the other two had to ask "yes-no" questions to find out who the famous person was. The fight started because Pamela said "yes" when she should have said "no". Pamela was thinking of Cleopatra and Denise asked her if she had blond hair. Pamela answered "yes". A few minutes later, after several more questions, Jenny guessed Cleopatra. Immediately Denise told Pamela that Cleopatra had dark hair, not blond hair. Pamela said she didn't care what color her hair was and she called Denise an idiot. Denise never liked to argue or fight, but she was tired of Pamela always wanting to be the boss. She called Pamela an idiot too and started to go home. When she turned around to leave, Pamela pushed her to the ground and started hitting her. Jenny ran into her house to get her mother. In less than a minute, Jenny's mother had separated the two girls. Denise's nose was bleeding and Pamela's dress was torn. Jenny's mother told them both to shake hands and to go home. They did what Jenny's mother said, but they didn't speak to each other. Denise went home after Jenny's mother had given her a handkerchief to stop the bleeding. That night, Pamela called Denise to apologize. She said that her mother had told her that Cleopatra had dark hair. Pamela wanted to apologize because the week before, Denise had invited her to go to the amusement park on Saturday with some friends and Pamela didn't want to miss the fun.

36. DENISE JOHNSON

1. Who did Denise have a fight with?
2. When did it happen?
3. Where did it happen?
4. Where does Jenny live?
5. What kind of game were the girls playing?
6. Were the rules simple or complicated?
7. What did the leader of the game have to think of?
8. What did the other two girls have to guess?
9. What kind of questions did they have to ask?
10. Who was Pamela thinking of?
11. What did Denise ask about Cleopatra?
12. How did Pamela answer?
13. How should she have answered?
14. Who finally guessed who the famous person was?
15. What did Denise say to Pamela about Cleopatra?
16. What was Pamela's response?
17. What did she call Denise?
18. What is it that Denise never liked to do?
19. What was she tired of?
20. What did she call Pamela?
21. Where did she start to go after calling Pamela an idiot?
22. What happened when she turned around to leave?
23. Where did Jenny, the other girl, go when they started fighting?
24. How soon did Jenny's mother come out?
25. How did she stop the fight?
26. What was Denise's condition after the fight?
27. What was Pamela's condition?
28. What did she tell them to do?
29. What did she give Denise?
30. Why did she give her a handkerchief?
31. What did Pamela do later that night?
32. What did she call Denise to do?
33. Did Pamela know that Denise had been right about Cleopatra?
34. How did she find out that Denise was right?
35. What was the real reason that Pamela called to apologize?
36. When had Denise invited her to the amusement park?

37. RONNY PERKINS

Ronny Perkins lives in Monte Carlo in a flat that costs more money to rent than he earns. Although he would love to be independent from his father, Nigel Perkins, he always ends up having to ask him for money to maintain the standard of living that he likes. Ronny owns a yacht that he bought two years ago with money his father lent him. During the summer months, when the weather is nice, he rents his yacht to people who want to cruise around the Gulf of Lyon, all the way to the Balearic Islands. Ronny makes quite a bit of money during the summer, but by Christmas, he has usually spent all of it on fine dinners and lots of drinks. He's well known around Monte Carlo as a kind of playboy but no one lets him buy on credit. Nigel doesn't know what to do with the boy. He's already 30 years old and he doesn't seem to be going anywhere. Ronny, however, has his own ideas. He's trying to convince a rich family in Corsica to finance the purchase of four yachts, two for the Gulf of Lyon and two for the Canary Islands, where it's summertime all year round. The only problem Ronny sees in the deal is that the family from Corsica has a lot of strange businesses. Some rumors say that the family has connections with the Mafia. The head of the family, Giuseppe Turqui, has agreed to lend Ronny $400,000 to buy a yacht and will rent him two other yachts that belong to the family. Ronny hasn't told Nigel anything about the business deal, which he's been working on for over eight months.

37. RONNY PERKINS

1. Where does Ronny Perkins live?
2. Does he live in a flat or in a house?
3. Does he live in a cheap flat?
4. What can you say about the cost of the rent?
5. Why can't Ronny become independent from his father?
6. Why does he need a lot of money?
7. Does Ronny own a yacht?
8. Where did he get the money to buy the yacht?
9. Did his father give him the money or lend it to him?
10. When does he rent the yacht to people?
11. Why does he rent it only during certain months?
12. Where do the people cruise on the yacht?
13. How much money does Ronny earn in the summer?
14. When does he usually run out of money?
15. What does he spend his money on?
16. What is he well known in Monte Carlo for?
17. What don't the people in Monte Carlo let him do?
18. What is Nigel's attitude concerning his son?
19. How old is Ronny?
20. What does Nigel think about Ronny's professional path?
21. What is Ronny doing regarding a rich family?
22. Where is this family from?
23. What does Ronny want to do with the four yachts?
24. Why does he want to locate two of the yachts in the Canary Islands?
25. What is Ronny worried about?
26. What has he heard about the family?
27. How much money has Giuseppe Turqui agreed to lend him?
28. What will Mr. Turqui rent to him?
29. What does Nigel know about his son's new business?
30. How long has Ronny been preparing this business deal?

38. MICHAEL JOHNSON

Michael turned 15 last Saturday. He received four presents from his parents and three other presents from relatives. However, his biggest birthday surprise was when he woke up on Saturday morning. His father came into his room and woke him up. He showed him the front page of the sports section in the Lincoln newspaper. There, in the middle of the page, was a photo of Michael shooting a free throw. It took the boy about five seconds to wake up completely and realize what was happening. Then he remembered the big game the night before. His middle school team had beaten the Omaha Buffaloes 79 to 66. It was a surprise to everyone and Michael had scored 34 points. His father was proud of his son. He had never seen Michael play so well. He seemed to control the game. However, for Michael, his 34 points weren't the most important thing for him. He had held Ricky Tanner, the star of the Omaha Buffaloes, to only 12 points. Ricky had achieved an average of 36 points a game during the season and was considered the best young basketball player in the state of Nebraska. Michael's strategy was to follow his coach's advice. His advice was to pay no attention to the ball when playing defense, but to concentrate only on Ricky Tanner and follow him everywhere. Michael had the advantage that he was faster than Ricky Tanner, so he stayed with him everywhere on the basketball court. This was suffocating for Ricky and disastrous for his team. Michael's defensive effort had broken the Buffaloes' strategy.

38. MICHAEL JOHNSON

1. When did Michael turn 15?
2. How many presents did he get from his parents?
3. How many presents did he get from other relatives?
4. Who woke him up on Saturday morning?
5. What did his father show him when he woke him up?
6. What was in the middle of the front page?
7. What was Michael doing in the photo?
8. How long did it take Michael to wake up completely?
9. What did he remember when he finally woke up?
10. What had happened the night before?
11. What was the final score of the game?
12. Was Michael's team favored to win the game?
13. How many points did Michael score?
14. What did Michael's father feel about his son?
15. Had he seen Michael play better in previous games?
16. How did Michael seem to his father during the game?
17. What was the most important thing for Michael?
18. Who was Ricky Tanner?
19. How many points per game did Ricky usually score?
20. What was Ricky considered by basketball experts?
21. How many points did he score last night?
22. Whose advice did Michael follow concerning Ricky?
23. What was the coach's advice?
24. What advantage did Michael have over Ricky?
25. Who did Michael concentrate on when playing defense?
26. What was the result for Ricky Tanner and his team?

39. PHILLIP JOHNSON

Phillip Johnson is lying in bed, thinking about George Clooney. His wife, Nancy, is still in the kitchen, washing dishes. Half an hour ago, Nancy told him about the offer from Eddie Campbell to decorate George Clooney's home in Aspen, Colorado. He's not worried about George Clooney. The guy must be around 50 by now and besides, he heard that up close George Clooney is not that handsome. What worries him, however, is that if Nancy does a good job on Clooney's home, she'll probably start getting other offers of a similar type. A lot of Hollywood stars own homes in Aspen and Phillip could imagine Nancy getting involved in a lot of work up there. On the other hand, it might be a good opportunity for him too. Even though he's the general manager of the Lincoln Bank, he's not a member of the Board of Directors. In many cases he doesn't have the final decision. Sometimes he feels more like a glorified employee than a real decision-maker. And besides, he hates having to travel to Omaha all the time. The bank has several difficult clients there and Phillip always has to argue with them about payments. He may be able to find a job in a bank in Aspen. The town is quite big. In high season, there must be at least 50,000 people living there and they need bank accounts like everybody else. He could probably get a good job in a local bank or maybe he could get an even better job in a Denver bank. Denver is only three hours from Aspen and maybe Nancy could work out of Denver instead of living in Aspen. Denver would also be a good city for Michael. Basketball in Colorado is even more competitive than in Nebraska. Maybe he's counting his chickens before they hatch. In any case, he'll tell Nancy that he supports her one hundred percent.

39. PHILLIP JOHNSON

1. Where is Phillip Johnson right now?
2. Who is he thinking about?
3. What is his wife doing right now?
4. What did Nancy tell him about earlier?
5. When did they have this conversation?
6. Is he worried about George Clooney?
7. How old must the guy be by now?
8. What do people say about George Clooney's looks?
9. What is Phillip worried about if Nancy does a good job on Clooney's home?
10. Who owns a lot of homes in Aspen, Colorado?
11. What could he imagine Nancy getting involved in?
12. Does he see an opportunity in it?
13. What's Phillip's position in the bank?
14. Is he a member of the Board?
15. What can't he do in many cases?
16. Does he feel he's a real decision-maker?
17. What does he feel like sometimes?
18. Where does he hate going?
19. Why does he hate going to Omaha?
20. Where does he think he might be able to find a job?
21. What can you say about the size of Aspen?
22. When are there more people in Aspen?
23. When is the population of Aspen at its highest?
24. What do these people need in Phillip's opinion?
25. Where does he think he could probably get a job?
26. Where does he think he could get an even better job?
27. How far is it from Denver to Aspen?
28. Why does Phillip think Denver would be a good place for Michael?
29. Is Phillip thinking rationally or counting his chickens before they hatch?
30. What has he decided to say to Nancy?

40. NIGEL PERKINS

Nigel Perkins has achieved another success. His company has just presented proof of a crime. Three months ago, a large insurance company asked Nigel's firm to investigate the death of a 62 year-old man. The man had died of a heart attack in strange circumstances. His wife, a 32 year-old ex-model had received seven million dollars from the insurance company. The man who died had been a friend of Nigel's and Nigel had personally supervised the investigation of the case. It turns out that the wife knew her husband suffered from poor blood circulation. Over a period of five months, she went to nine different pharmacies to file a prescription for hemophiliacs. The drug she bought made her husband's blood circulation even worse and eventually he died. On the request of the insurance company, Nigel's firm investigated the woman. First they discovered that she was having an affair with a doctor. Second, they went through at least one ton of garbage in the basement of the building where she lived. After 10 days, they found a prescription in the garbage for the medicine in question. They found the name of the same doctor on it and then contacted the distributors of the medicine. Finally, they visited 27 pharmacies in the general area where the woman lived. Employees in four different pharmacies recognized her from a photograph. At that point, Nigel's firm contacted the police. The woman was called in for interrogation but she denied everything. However, when the police contacted the doctor, he confessed to the crime. Now he and the ex-model are in prison awaiting trial and six of the seven million dollars have been recovered.

40. NIGEL PERKINS

1. What has Nigel Perkins achieved?
2. What has his company just presented?
3. What did the insurance company ask Nigel to do?
4. When did they ask him to investigate the case?
5. How old was the man who died?
6. How old was his wife?
7. What did she use to do for a living?
8. How did the man die?
9. How much money did his wife receive from the insurance company?
10. What had Nigel's relationship been with the man who had died?
11. What was Nigel's role in the investigation?
12. What did the wife know about her husband's health?
13. How many pharmacies did she visit?
14. Over what period of time did she visit the pharmacies?
15. What did the drug she bought do to her husband's blood circulation?
16. What was the medicine for?
17. What was the first thing Nigel's company discovered?
18. Did the woman live in a house or a flat?
19. What did Nigel's firm do in her block of flats?
20. Where was the garbage located in the building?
21. How much garbage did the company search through?
22. What did they finally find?
23. How long did it take them to find the prescription?
24. Whose name was on the prescription?
25. Who did they contact before visiting the pharmacies?
26. How many pharmacies did they visit?
27. Which pharmacies did they visit?
28. How many pharmacy employees recognized the woman in a picture?
29. What did Nigel's firm do after that?
30. Who did the police interrogate first?
31. Did she confess or did she deny everything?
32. Who did they interrogate next?
33. Did he confess or deny everything?
34. Where are the doctor and the woman now?
35. What are they awaiting?
36. How much of the money has been recovered?

41. AKI MORITA

Aki Morita feels relieved. Ten minutes ago, he gave his wife what he thought would be bad news: their transfer to Louisiana. He and his wife hardly ever speak about Aki's work. In fact, they hardly ever have time to talk to each other. This evening, however, they talked for at least 15 minutes, and Aki was surprised that his wife knew 10 times more about Louisiana than he did. She knew about Baton Rouge, New Orleans, and even Natchez, where the plantation homes are located. Aki's wife spends a lot of time alone at home. She likes to read and three months ago she read a novel about the saga of a rich Louisiana family before and during the American Civil War. She explained to her husband the history of Louisiana during that period and about the way of life in Louisiana. Aki couldn't believe it. When he told her that they would probably spend at least three years there, she said that it would be a good opportunity for the children to learn English well. What she didn't tell him was what she had heard from other wives whose husbands work for Honda. She had heard that Japanese families who are transferred to Europe or America lead a very good life. They receive a special allowance that almost doubles the husband's salary. Aki's wife is very familiar with life in the United States because she reads at least four American novels every year. She has a romantic vision of the country.

41. AKI MORITA

1. How does Aki feel right now?
2. What news has he just given his wife?
3. How long ago did he tell her?
4. Did he expect the news to be good or bad?
5. What do he and his wife hardly ever talk about?
6. Why don't they talk to each other very much?
7. How long did they talk this evening?
8. Why was Aki surprised?
9. How much more does his wife know about Louisiana than he does?
10. What three cities in Louisiana did she know about?
11. What is located in Natchez?
12. What does Aki's wife spend a lot of time doing?
13. When did she read a novel about Louisiana?
14. What was the novel about?
15. What did Aki's wife explain to her husband?
16. What was Aki's reaction?
17. What did he tell her about the duration of their stay in Louisiana?
18. Was she upset?
19. Who did she think it would be a good opportunity for?
20. Why would it be a good opportunity for them?
21. What had she heard from other Honda wives?
22. What is the real salary of a Honda executive in Europe or America?
23. Why is it almost double?
24. Why is Aki's wife so familiar with American life?
25. What kind of vision does she have of the U.S.?

42. INÉS GARCÍA

Inés García is back in Seville today, working at her father's law firm. However, her mind is still on Paris, where she has just spent four days with François Monet. She had been to Paris once before, but that was when she was a little girl. She only remembered the Eiffel Tower and Notre Dame from that visit. This time, however, François took her to all the popular sights and to several charming and "secret" places. The highlight of her visit was simply the hour she spent in a rowboat with François in the Boulogne Forest just outside of Paris. It was a lovely day and they had a lovely time. Before she left for Seville on Sunday, François told her that he was falling in love. She didn't say anything because she didn't want him to know that she was absolutely crazy about him. On the flight back, she made the decision to break up with her boyfriend in Seville. She decided that she would tell him everything. It would be hard for him but it was the best thing to do. They had been together for four years, and for Inés, the relationship had been fun but not passionate. She had never met anyone like François, and she was experiencing a feeling she had never known before. She was convinced that she had finally met Mr. Right.

42. INÉS GARCÍA

1. Where is Inés today?
2. Is this her first day back in Seville or was she there during the weekend?
3. Where was she during the weekend?
4. How many days was she there?
5. Who did she spend the four days with?
6. How many times had she been to Paris before?
7. When did she go there?
8. What things did she remember from that visit?
9. Where did François take her?
10. What was the highlight of her visit?
11. Where is the Boulogne Forest?
12. How was the weather that day?
13. What kind of time did they have together?
14. What day did she return to Seville?
15. What did François tell her before she left?
16. What did she say to him?
17. What didn't she want him to know yet?
18. What decision did she make concerning her boyfriend in Seville?
19. Where did she make this decision?
20. What did she decide she would tell him?
21. How did she think he would react?
22. How long had they been together?
23. Describe how Inés considered their relationship.
24. Had she ever met anyone like François?
25. What kind of feeling was she experiencing?
26. What was she convinced of?

43. PAULA EISENBACH

Paula Eisenbach is glad she has only one more semester before she finishes her studies. Although she loves Heidelberg, she wants to get away from it. Right now she's sunbathing on a long beach in the Canary Islands. She's with her parents, away from the university and away from Tom Sanders. Her last two weeks in Heidelberg were unbearable. Ever since she told Tom she wasn't interested in going with him to California, he's been calling her. He calls her at least three times a day. Twice Paula has seen him following her between the university buildings. Her two flat-mates told her she should call the police, but Paula doesn't think it's necessary. She thinks Tom will eventually get over his infatuation with her and leave her alone. If he continues harassing her when she gets back to Heidelberg in January, then she may go to the police. Tom's a strange young man. He's a very talented artist but he's extremely introverted. He never does anything but work on his drawings and talk about how he hates the food in Germany. His apartment is always messy and he always wears either the same blue suit without a tie or a Disneyland T-shirt. He never goes out and doesn't seem to have any friends. She worked at his apartment for about two months and he never asked her out to dinner or even to have a coffee. For the next two weeks, however, Paula can forget about Tom and enjoy the sun and the beach. She'll spend another week with her parents in Munich before heading back to Heidelberg. By then, hopefully Tom will have found another person to help him and will have forgotten about Paula.

43. PAULA EISENBACH

1. What is Paula glad about?
2. What is her feeling about Heidelberg?
3. What is she doing right now?
4. Who is she with?
5. How were her last two weeks in Heidelberg?
6. What has Tom Sanders been doing since she told him she wasn't going to California with him?
7. How many times a day does he call her?
8. What else has Paula seen him doing?
9. How many times has she seen him following her?
10. Where has she seen him following her?
11. What did her flat-mates tell her she should do?
12. What does Paula think about this?
13. What does she think Tom will eventually do?
14. What might she do if he continues harassing her when she gets back to university?
15. When will she get back to university?
16. What kind of man is Tom?
17. What kind of artist is he?
18. What kind of person is he psychologically?
19. What are the only two things he normally does?
20. What is the usual condition of his apartment?
21. What does Tom always wear?
22. How often does he go out?
23. How many friends does he have?
24. How long did Paula work with Tom at his apartment?
25. How many times did he ask her out to dinner?
26. How many times did they go out for a coffee?
27. What can Paula do for the next two weeks in the Canary Islands?
28. Where will she go after her two weeks there?
29. How long will she be with her parents in Munich?
30. Where will she go after that?
31. What does she hope Tom will have found by then?
32. Who does she hope he will have forgotten about?

Pierre Monet had to stay at the Ministry yesterday until 7:00 p.m. He was asked to work with a colleague to translate a secret document that had arrived just before 4:00 p.m. from the French Embassy in London. Pierre usually goes home at 4:00, but his boss rushed into Pierre's office just as he was getting ready to leave. He told him that the President of the Republic needed the document translated immediately. When Pierre called his wife to tell her that he'd be late, she told him that he had just received at home a 15-page report from the Chairman of Peugeot and that it had to be done by 9:00 a.m. the next morning. Pierre told his wife he'd be home around 8:00 p.m. and that he'd probably need no more than two hours to do the translation. After hanging up, he and a colleague of his divided up the 23-page document from the French Embassy and started working on it. It was a secret report from the British Ministry of Defense to the Prime Minister. Pierre wondered how the report had found its way to the French Embassy, but that was really none of his business. The report was about the British position concerning the construction of a new Eurofighter attack jet to be constructed by a consortium of companies in the U.K., France, Germany and Spain. In the report, the British Minister of Defense was complaining about the French and the Germans. In his opinion, the U.K. and Spain were not being included in some of the sensitive meetings and decisions. The report gave a list of meetings that had taken place between the French and German companies without the knowledge of the other two partners. The Minister concluded the report recommending that this subject be included in the informal meeting scheduled between the Prime Minister and the French President during the next NATO meeting in Brussels.

44. PIERRE MONET

1. How late did Pierre Monet have to stay at the Ministry yesterday?
2. What was he asked to do?
3. Who was he asked to work with?
4. What time did the document arrive?
5. Where did it arrive from?
6. What time does Pierre usually go home?
7. Who asked him to stay longer?
8. Did his boss walk calmly into Pierre's office?
9. How did he enter Pierre's office?
10. What was Pierre getting ready to do when his boss rushed into his office?
11. Who needed the document translated?
12. How soon did the President need the translation?
13. Who did Pierre call?
14. What did he tell her?
15. What did she tell him?
16. When did this translation need to be ready?
17. What time did Pierre tell his wife he'd be home?
18. How long did he tell her he'd need to do the Peugeot translation?
19. How long was the translation from Peugeot?
20. How long was the translation from the French Embassy?
21. Did Pierre do it himself or did he divide it up with a colleague?
22. What did Pierre wonder about the document?
23. Was this an important concern for him or was it really none of his business?
24. Who was the document from?
25. Who was it addressed to?
26. What was it about?
27. What countries were involved in the construction of the Eurofighter?
28. Who did the British Minister of Defense complain about in the report?
29. What was his complaint?
30. What kind of list did the report include?
31. What did the Minister recommend at the end of the report?
32. When was the next meeting between the British Prime Minister and the French President?
33. Was it supposed to be a formal or informal meeting?
34. Where was it going to take place?
35. Why was it going to take place in Brussels?

45. NATASHA ZARAKOVICH

Natasha Zarakovich thought she knew English well. However, her first two days in Scotland have made her think otherwise. She arrived on Friday, the 22nd and spent Saturday and Sunday with her cousin, André, and his family. In the evenings she went out with André and a group of friends. She didn't have any trouble understanding the family, because they spoke Russian, or English with a slight Russian accent. But the evenings were different. She had a lot of trouble understanding André's friends. She had to make a big effort every time they said something to her. What made things worse was that they went to a noisy restaurant and then to a discotheque. Natasha felt embarrassed because she kept having to ask the friends to repeat everything. Later André told her not to worry about it. He knew that by the time she left for Moscow in early January, she would understand everyone quite well. On Saturday afternoon, after lunch, André took Natasha to Edinburgh, the capital of Scotland. She had never seen such a beautiful city. She spent more than half an hour standing in Princes Street looking across at the castle of Mary, Queen of Scots. It was a cold and windy day, and André wanted to go inside a pub to get warm. However, Natasha was used to the Russian winters and the weather seemed almost warm to her. Everything was so different to her. She had never been more than 50 kilometers outside of Moscow in her life. Here, there were cars everywhere, coming and going. Everyone seemed to be in a hurry. André told her that compared to London, Edinburgh and Glasgow were quiet cities. He also told her that they would be going to London in a few days to see the sights and to go to a musical; either "Cats" or "The Phantom of the Opera".

45. NATASHA ZARAKOVICH

1. Where is Natasha Zarakovich now?
2. What did she think she knew?
3. What made her think otherwise?
4. When did she arrive in Scotland?
5. Who did she spend Saturday and Sunday with?
6. What did she do in the evenings?
7. Did she have trouble understanding the family?
8. Why not?
9. Who did she have trouble understanding?
10. What kind of effort did she have to make to understand them?
11. What made things worse?
12. Why did she feel embarrassed?
13. What did André tell her later about this problem?
14. What did André think about how Natasha would progress with her English?
15. When would Natasha leave for Moscow?
16. Where did André take her on Saturday afternoon?
17. What is Edinburgh in Scotland?
18. What was Natasha's reaction to Edinburgh?
19. How long was she standing in Princes Street?
20. Why did she spend so much time there?
21. What was the weather like?
22. What did André want to do because of the weather?
23. Did Natasha feel cold?
24. Why didn't she feel cold?
25. How did Natasha find things compared to Moscow?
26. How far had she been outside of Moscow?
27. What did she see everywhere?
28. What was her impression of the people?
29. How did André compare Edinburgh and Glasgow to London?
30. When did he say they would be going to London?
31. What two things would they do in London?
32. What musical would they see?

46. LI TONG

Last night Li Tong was thinking about giving up the idea of learning English. He had already attended six classes but he still couldn't understand a word the teacher was saying. He felt embarrassed in class because most of the students seemed to be progressing quite well. He had the impression that he was holding back the class. However, thanks to his daughter, he changed his mind before going to bed. It turns out that when he told his wife that he was thinking about giving up, his daughter was doing her homework at the kitchen table. When she heard her father say this, she got up and told him that English was easy. She showed him her English book and, together, they studied the first two chapters. Li had always thought that his daughter was a gifted child and now he was sure of it. She explained to him how to conjugate the verb "to be" in the singular and the plural; and in the first, second and third person. Then she asked him questions using the interrogative form. Li was impressed. His daughter was only eight years old and she was teaching English better than his English teacher. They practiced the structures in the first two chapters for over 30 minutes. That night, when he went to bed, Li made a resolution to continue studying the language and to make a bigger effort to understand what the teacher and the other students were saying in class.

46. LI TONG

1. What was Li Tong thinking about doing last night?
2. How many classes had he already attended?
3. What couldn't he still understand?
4. How did he feel in class?
5. Why did he feel embarrassed?
6. What kind of impression did he have?
7. Thanks to whom did he change his mind?
8. Who did he talk to at home about giving up the classes?
9. Who heard him tell his wife this?
10. What was his daughter doing when she heard her father talking to his wife?
11. Where was she doing her homework?
12. What did she do when she heard her father?
13. What did she show him?
14. What did they study together?
15. What kind of child had Li always thought his daughter was?
16. What was he sure about now?
17. What did his daughter explain to him?
18. What kind of questions did she ask him?
19. How did Li react to his daughter's actions?
20. How old is his daughter?
21. What was his opinion of her as a teacher?
22. How long did they practice the first two chapters?
23. What resolution did Li make?
24. When did he make this resolution?

47. ANNA BARGHINI

Anna Barghini is on her way to Stuttgart. She's flying business class and thinking about Karl Polster. She had never thought she would like a German man... not even in her wildest dreams. However, just yesterday she received a letter from Karl. In it, he told her the truth. The letter was only three paragraphs long, but Karl must have spent hours working on it because it certainly made a strong and pleasant impression on Anna. First he told her that he wasn't the type of person to insinuate his feelings to anyone. He admitted that he was very fond of her and that he couldn't stop thinking about her. Secondly, he told her that she was one of the most attractive and intelligent women he had ever met and that, logically, he had been deeply affected by her presence. Thirdly, he told her that he knew very well that her family was wealthy, but he assured her that money was not, and had never been, a factor that influenced his feelings toward people. He was from an upper-middle class family that had a small, but comfortable estate and he was not ambitious to amass a fortune. Finally, he asked her to have dinner with him her first night in Stuttgart in a small restaurant in the center of town where he liked to go when he wanted to enjoy a long, pleasant meal. His uncle owns the restaurant and it serves the best Alsatian cuisine he has ever tasted. When Anna finished reading the letter, she sat still for a moment. She had never received such a warm, sincere letter in her life. Maybe she ought to get to know this Karl Polster fellow a little better.

47. ANNA BARGHINI

1. What city is Anna Barghini on her way to?
2. Is she going there by plane or by train?
3. Is she flying tourist class or business class?
4. Who is she thinking about?
5. What kind of man did she think she would never like?
6. What did she receive just yesterday?
7. Did Karl tell her his true feelings in the letter?
8. How long was the letter?
9. How long did Karl probably spend writing it?
10. What kind of impression did it make on Anna?
11. What type of person did Karl tell her he wasn't?
12. What did he admit?
13. Who did he say he couldn't stop thinking about?
14. What did he say about her qualities?
15. How had he been affected by her presence?
16. What did he say he knew about her family?
17. What did he assure her concerning money?
18. What can you say about Karl's family?
19. What did Karl say about his ambitions?
20. What did he ask her to do with him on her first night in Stuttgart?
21. Where did he invite her to have dinner?
22. Who owns the restaurant?
23. What kind of food does it serve?
24. What is Karl's opinion of the food?
25. What did Anna do after reading the letter from Karl?
26. What hadn't Anna ever received?
27. What did she decide she ought to do?

48. NANCY JOHNSON

Last Friday Nancy Johnson and her husband, Phillip, took the day off to drive to Denver, Colorado. They drove across almost all of Nebraska and half of Colorado. It took them nine hours. They spent Friday night at the Marriot Hotel. The next morning, they drove up to Aspen, along endless, winding roads. They had lunch there and then Nancy took the car and drove to the house George Clooney had bought. When she got there, she saw a man with a shovel clearing a path to the front door through the snow. The man didn't notice that Nancy had arrived. As she walked up to the man, along the path he had cleared, she asked him if Mr. Clooney was in. Apparently she scared him because he was so busy clearing the snow that he hadn't heard her come up to him from behind. When he turned around, he smiled and said "yes". Nancy stood frozen. It was George Clooney himself. She had thought the man was a gardener or someone similar. All she could manage to say was her name. Apparently, Mr. Clooney was used to this and he smiled and invited her into the house to have a coffee. When Nancy went into the house, she immediately realized that no one had lived there for a long time. It was cold, dirty and empty. They went into the kitchen where Mr. Clooney had an electric heater on. He poured her a coffee and one for himself and then they sat down at an old wooden table. One of the table legs was shorter than the other three and the table kept moving whenever either one of them leaned on it. However, Nancy didn't even realize it. She was thinking about her hair and her clothes. Mr. Clooney was wearing a pair of old blue jeans and a flannel shirt. He didn't seem to care about anything.

48. NANCY JOHNSON

1. What day did Nancy and Phillip take off last week?
2. What did they take Friday off to do?
3. Which two states did they drive across?
4. How long did it take them to drive to Denver?
5. What hotel did they stay at on Friday night?
6. Where did they drive the next morning?
7. What can you say about the roads to Aspen?
8. Where did they have lunch?
9. Who took the car after lunch?
10. Where did she drive?
11. Did she see a man or a woman when she got there?
12. What was the man holding?
13. What was he doing?
14. Did he see her arrive?
15. What did Nancy ask the man?
16. Why did she scare him?
17. What did he do when he turned around to Nancy?
18. Who was the man?
19. What did Nancy do when she realized who it was?
20. Who had she thought the man was?
21. What was the only thing Nancy could manage to say?
22. Was George Clooney used to this kind of reaction or did he think Nancy was a little strange?
23. What did he invite her to do?
24. What did Nancy realize when she entered the house?
25. What was the house like?
26. What part of the house did they go to?
27. Why was the kitchen warm?
28. How many coffees did George Clooney pour?
29. Where did they sit down?
30. What was the problem with the table?
31. Why didn't Nancy notice the problem?
32. What was George Clooney wearing?

49. LUIGI BARGHINI

Luigi Barghini is escorting three engineers from Mercedes Benz around his factory in Verona. He's showing them the different steps in the manufacturing process. Earlier in the morning, he, Anna, and the Technical Director of the company spent two hours with the engineers in the meeting room next to Luigi's office. They went over every detail of a supply agreement. The Technical Director described the raw materials used in making the car seats and the aluminum used for the frames. Anna spoke about the company's fine record in deliveries and in quality assurance. Finally, Luigi explained how the car seats would be shipped to Stuttgart. However, Dieter Mittelmann, the Chief Engineer, didn't seem convinced. He had never worked with an Italian supplier and he was afraid that strikes could delay shipments and cause production problems in Germany. Anna assured him that the company had suffered only one strike in ten years. It had been a general strike throughout Italy and it had lasted only two days. She went on to explain that the factory workers and employees in the company were paid well above the going rate in the area and in the automotive industry. Luigi added that he spent a lot of time with the workers and was proud of the spirit and collaboration on the factory floor. Finally, the Technical Director showed the three Germans four different awards the company had received from different customers for the quality of their work. Two of the awards were from Fiat, one from Volvo, and another from Rover, which was now owned by BMW. The German chief engineer looked at them but didn't say anything.

49. LUIGI BARGHINI

1. Where is Luigi now?
2. What is he doing?
3. What is he showing the German engineers?
4. What happened earlier in the morning?
5. How many people attended the meeting?
6. Who attended the meeting from Luigi's company?
7. What did they go over in the meeting?
8. What did the technical director describe?
9. What did Anna Barghini speak about?
10. What did Luigi explain?
11. Who is Dieter Mittelmann?
12. What was his attitude during the meeting?
13. What was he worried about?
14. What did Anna assure him of?
15. What kind of strike was it?
16. How long had it lasted?
17. What did Anna explain about the workers' pay?
18. What did Luigi add about the workers?
19. What did the Technical Director show the Germans?
20. What were the awards for?
21. What company were two of the awards from?
22. What other two companies had given them an award?
23. How did the German Chief Engineer react to this?

50. RONNY PERKINS

Ronny Perkins is concerned about his new business. Three months ago, with the help of the Turqui family from Corsica, he was able to acquire three new yachts. With these three yachts, and the one he already owned, Ronny was able to expand his business from one to two yachts in the Gulf of Lyon and to start up a new business in the Canary Islands with the other two yachts. The problem is he doesn't trust the Turqui family, especially Giuseppe's son, Carlo. Originally, the Turqui family was only going to give Ronny a loan to buy one yacht and to rent him two more. However, in the end, the family gave him all three yachts in exchange for 50 percent of Ronny's company. Ronny couldn't do anything about it because he wasn't in a position to negotiate. In addition, Giuseppe insisted that his son, Carlo, would be the assistant manager to look after the family's 50 percent. Now Carlo is talking about increasing the capital of the company in order to buy eight new yachts to expand the business even more. The total cost of these yachts amounts to over three million dollars. Ronny, of course, doesn't have 1.5 million dollars to maintain his 50 % share of the business. He sees that gradually the Turqui family is going to take over his company. He doesn't know it, but one month ago Nigel sent a member of his private investigation agency to Monte Carlo and Corsica to look into the Turqui family and to look into Ronny's finances as well. Even though Ronny had never mentioned the Corsica connection, a friend of Nigel's in the London offices of Barclays Bank had heard about the business deal from the manager of Barclay's operations in Monaco.

50. RONNY PERKINS

1. What is Ronny Perkins concerned about?
2. What did he acquire three months ago?
3. Who helped him acquire the yachts?
4. How many yachts does he have in all?
5. How many yachts does he operate in the Gulf of Lyon?
6. Where else has he started operations?
7. How many yachts does he have in the Canary Islands?
8. Who doesn't Ronny trust?
9. Who especially doesn't he trust?
10. What was the original agreement between Ronny and the Turqui family?
11. In the end, what did the family do?
12. What percentage of the business did they acquire?
13. Why couldn't Ronny do anything?
14. What is Carlo talking about now?
15. What does he want to use the capital increase for?
16. What would the total cost of the new yachts amount to?
17. What problem will Ronny have if the company increases its capital to more than 3 million dollars?
18. What does he think the Turqui family is gradually going to do?
19. Where did Nigel send a member of his company?
20. When did he send him there?
21. Does Ronny know about this?
22. What did Nigel tell the detective to do?
23. Had Ronny mentioned the Turqui family to Nigel?
24. How did Nigel find out about the Corsica connection?

51. AKI MORITA

Aki Morita and his family have been in Baton Rouge, Louisiana for two months. Aki hasn't changed his habits. He still goes to work before 7:00 a.m. and gets back home just before dinner time. However, dinner time in Louisiana is 6:00 p.m., but Aki and his family still have dinner around 8:00. When Aki arrived, the new Honda factory was three months away from completion. The works are on schedule and production should start within six weeks. Aki is busy making contact with suppliers and training the factory personnel on the Honda quality procedures. He desperately needs more people in his department to evaluate the American suppliers who are bidding on supply contracts. A Japanese colleague of his is in charge of purchasing and the two are working together. Fortunately, the other man has been living in the States for two years and knows more about how things work. However, Aki is learning fast. His English is improving tremendously and he is finally starting to understand the strange southern accent spoken by the people in Louisiana. Aki's wife is enjoying her new life for the moment. She's made friends with the purchasing manager's wife, who is an American from a small town in Texas called Bertram. The woman wants to learn Japanese and Aki's wife has agreed to give her classes for free. They live on the same block and always go shopping together. Aki's wife loves to shop at the nearby mall. There must be more than 200 different shops there and the prices are not bad. Aki's salary in Louisiana is almost double what he earned in Japan. The only problem seems to be the kids. They're having some trouble adapting to the American school system. The subjects are easy for them, but the language barrier is still a problem. However, they're young and they'll soon learn to speak English as well as Japanese.

51. AKI MORITA

1. How long have Aki and his family been in Louisiana?

2. Has Aki already changed his working habits?

3. What time does he leave home in the morning?

4. When does he get back home in the evening?

5. What time do people have dinner in Louisiana?

6. What time do Aki and his family have dinner?

7. How close to completion was the Honda factory when Aki arrived in Louisiana?

8. Is the construction work on schedule or behind schedule?

9. When should production start?

10. What is Aki busy doing?

11. What does he desperately need?

12. What does he need these people for?

13. What is the other Japanese colleague in charge of?

14. What advantage does the other man have over Aki?

15. What can you say about Aki's English?

16. What is he finally starting to understand?

17. How is Aki's wife doing?

18. Who has she made friends with?

19. What nationality is she?

20. Where is she from?

21. What does the woman want to learn?

22. What has Aki's wife agreed to do with the woman?

23. How much is she going to charge for the classes?

24. Where do the two families live relative to each other?

25. What do the two wives always do together?

26. Where does Aki's wife love to shop?

27. How far is the shopping mall from her house?

28. How many shops does Aki's wife think there must be in the mall?

29. What is her impression about the prices?

30. How much does Aki earn compared to Japan?

31. What seems to be the only problem?

32. What's the biggest problem?

33. What positive thing can you say about this problem?

52. PHILLIP JOHNSON

Phillip Johnson feels like the queen's consort. His wife, Nancy, has only been involved with George Clooney's house for three weeks and she's already a public figure in Lincoln, Nebraska. Her picture was on the front page of the local newspaper the day after the news got out. Now everyone at the bank is comparing Nancy to Demi Moore in the movie "Indecent Proposal", where Robert Redford paid Demi Moore a million dollars to spend the night with him. Phillip doesn't appreciate the jokes in the office, but he likes the idea of his wife earning almost a quarter of a million dollars for eight months' work. Of course, he sees her now only on Mondays and Tuesdays, the two days she takes off each week to be with the family in Lincoln. The rest of the time she lives and works in Aspen. She's renting a small apartment there where she's set up her design studio. She works on the weekends in Aspen because that's the only time George Clooney can get away from Los Angeles. Nancy finds him a delightful person to work with. He has good taste for decoration but he leaves most of the decisions up to her. Phillip isn't, by nature, a jealous person. However, Nancy is still very attractive for her age and working closely with George Clooney would be any woman's dream. For Phillip, the daily routine at the bank is starting to seem more and more tedious. He's bought a six-month subscription to the Denver Post, but he hasn't seen any decent job offers yet. Every night he talks with Nancy on the phone for about half an hour. The phone bill is surely going to amount to a lot of money, but it's worth it, he supposes. There are a lot of nice things the family can do with an extra 250,000 dollars.

52. PHILLIP JOHNSON

1. Who does Phillip Johnson feel like?
2. How long has Nancy been involved with George Clooney's house?
3. Why is she a public figure in Lincoln?
4. When was her photo published in the local newspaper?
5. Who is everyone at the bank comparing Nancy to?
6. What happened in the movie "Indecent Proposal"?
7. What does Phillip think about the jokes in the office?
8. What does he like about Nancy's new job?
9. How long will Nancy be involved in the project?
10. How often does Phillip see his wife now?
11. Why doesn't Nancy take the weekends off?
12. Where does Nancy live?
13. Has she bought an apartment or is she renting one?
14. What has she set up in her apartment?
15. What kind of person is George Clooney in Nancy's opinion?
16. What kind of taste does he have for decoration?
17. Does he make most of the decisions himself or does he leave them up to Nancy?
18. What can you say about Phillip in terms of jealousy?
19. What, however, is he worried about concerning his wife working with George Clooney?
20. How is Phillip starting to feel with regard to the daily routine at the bank in Lincoln?
21. What kind of subscription has he bought?
22. Why has he bought a subscription to the Denver Post?
23. How many good job offers has he seen so far?
24. How often does he talk with his wife on the phone?
25. How long are their conversations?
26. What does he think about the telephone bill?
27. Why does he think all the trouble is worth it?

53. INÉS GARCÍA

Inés García had never been so excited in her life. Ever since she had got back to Seville from Paris two months ago, she had talked to François Monet on the telephone almost every day. It's a good thing he usually called her, because otherwise her father might have said something to her about the phone bill. Two weeks ago, François surprised her with some unbelievable news. A week earlier, he had mentioned to his uncle Pierre Monet that he was looking for a way of bringing Inés to live in Paris. The next day, Pierre called him to say that he had asked the Chairman of Peugeot if they might need a lawyer expert in Spanish labor law. At first, the man had said no, but when Pierre explained the circumstances and told him that his nephew was love-sick, the benevolent side of the Chairman came out and he assured Pierre that Inés could come to work for Peugeot in the legal department. When François conveyed the message to Inés, she jumped for joy. She was tired of defending boring labor cases in Seville and was dying to be with François. He told her to prepare her C.V. and send it with a letter to the Chairman of Peugeot, thanking him for his fine gesture and saying something about herself. He gave her the address. The next morning, Inés called a friend of hers who had grown up in France and asked if she could help her write a letter and a C.V. in French. Two days later she sent them to Peugeot. Exactly seven days later, she received a nice letter from the head of Human Resources offering her an initial one-year contract to work as an assistant to the Chief Legal Counsel at Peugeot. He told her that she should be settled in Paris and ready to work within 30 days. For Inés, it was a dream come true. Her father thought it was wonderful. Her mother insisted that she wanted to meet this François Monet fellow before letting her daughter go off to Paris. When Inés told him this, François immediately reserved a ticket on Iberia to fly Paris-Madrid-Seville for the following weekend.

53. INÉS GARCÍA

1. How would you describe Inés' psychological state?
2. How long ago did she return from Paris?
3. How often had she spoken to François since she got back?
4. Who usually called whom?
5. Why did Inés think it was a good thing he called her most of the time?
6. What did François surprise her with two weeks ago?
7. Who had François spoken to about Inés?
8. When had he spoken to him about her?
9. What is Pierre's relationship to François?
10. What did François tell Pierre he was looking for?
11. Who did Pierre call the next day?
12. What did he ask the Chairman?
13. What was the Chairman's initial response?
14. What did Pierre go on to explain to him?
15. What kind of illness did he say his nephew had?
16. What side of the Chairman's character came out when Pierre told him his nephew was love-sick?
17. What did he assure Pierre?
18. What was Inés' reaction when François conveyed this message to her?
19. What was she tired of doing in Seville?
20. Who was she dying to see?
21. What did François tell her to prepare?
22. Did he tell her to send the CV directly to him?
23. Who did he tell her to send the CV to?
24. What else did he tell her to write?
25. What did he tell her to say in the letter?
26. Who did Inés call the next morning?
27. What did Inés ask her?
28. How many days later did she send the letter and CV?
29. How soon did she get a reply?
30. Who was the reply from?
31. What kind of contract did he offer her?
32. What would her job be in Peugeot?
33. When did he tell her she should be ready to work?
34. What did all this represent for Inés?
35. What did her father think about it?
36. What did her mother insist on?
37. What did François do when Inés told him about her mother's wish?
38. What airline did he reserve a ticket with?
39. What route would he fly?
40. When would he be in Seville?

54. KARL POLSTER

Karl Polster was sitting opposite Anna Barghini in a small, intimate restaurant in the center of Stuttgart. Even though he had "opened his heart" to Anna in a letter he had sent her the week before, he still felt self-conscious and unsure of himself with her. She was rich, beautiful, and the general manager of the second largest car seat manufacturer in Europe. What impressed him even more was that she was only 27. Of course, one could say that her wealth and corporate position were the result of having a rich father who owned a company. However, her beauty was hers and hers alone, and she had already won the respect of a lot of people at Mercedes Benz thanks to her keen business sense. Karl wanted so much to gain her affection that he couldn't help feeling nervous. He was 34 years old and hadn't had a serious relationship with a woman since he was 27. Back then, he was engaged to a girl from Hanover, but two months before they were supposed to be married, she died in a traffic accident. Since then, Karl had tried to forget the loss by devoting himself entirely to his job at Mercedes Benz. He had moved up the ranks in the company and was now the General Purchasing Director. He realized that his devotion to work had changed his personality and made him a much more serious person. That's why he was now having trouble connecting with Anna in a fun, natural way. During the dinner, he told her about the tragic events of seven years before, and how he had thrown himself into his work at the company. Anna said very little during most of the meal. However, she felt comfortable and at ease. Karl seemed like a sad person who was trying his best to be a pleasant host. He seemed sincere and she could see that he was very cultured.

54. KARL POLSTER

1. Who was Karl Polster sitting opposite?
2. Where were they having dinner?
3. Where was the restaurant?
4. What had Karl done in his letter to Anna?
5. When had he sent it to her?
6. How did he feel in front of her?
7. What qualities did Anna possess in Karl's eyes?
8. What impressed him even more?
9. What could one say concerning her wealth and corporate position?
10. What would one have to admit concerning her beauty?
11. What had she won among a lot of people at Mercedes Benz?
12. Why had she gained their respect?
13. What did Karl desperately want to gain from her?
14. What was it he couldn't keep from feeling?
15. Was Karl older than Anna?
16. How old was he?
17. How long had it been since he had had a serious relationship with a woman?
18. Who had he been engaged to seven years ago?
19. What happened to her?
20. When did the accident happen?
21. How many women had Karl had a relationship with since then?
22. What had he done to forget the loss of his fiancée?
23. What was his position now at Mercedes Benz?
24. What did he realize about his devotion to his job?
25. How did this affect his behavior in front of Anna?
26. What did he tell her during the dinner?
27. What was Anna's behavior during the dinner?
28. How did she feel with Karl?
29. What kind of person did Karl seem like to her?
30. What was her opinion about him as a person?

Michael Johnson turned 15 three weeks ago. He is now in his first year of high school. High school is where students do the last four years of secondary education before going to university. In some states in the U.S., it's the last three years of secondary education. Michael, however, is in a 4-year high school and is one of the youngest in the school. Most of the students seem a lot older and more mature than him. The school has two basketball teams, a junior team and a senior team. The basketball coach has started Michael practicing with the senior team despite his age. Michael's height is not a problem. He's 1 meter, 81 centimeters tall. The coach saw Michael play in three games last year when the boy was in middle school, including the state finals where he scored 34 points and held Ricky Tanner to only 12. He was so impressed that he thinks Michael might be able to play on the senior team. He's sure that by the time Michael turns 17, he could potentially become one of the best high school basketball players in the nation. He's never seen a boy so good in every aspect of the game. Right now, Michael is competing with three older boys for the position of point guard. He's definitely better than two of them, but the third, Dennis Fletcher, is an excellent shot. He never misses a basket. Last year he scored an average of 18 points a game on the senior team. Michael, however, is much faster than Dennis Fletcher and probably much better on defense. Maybe the coach could move Dennis Fletcher to another position. What Michael doesn't know is that the coach has already made the decision to start Dennis Fletcher in the first two games and to send in Michael in the second half. If Michael has any problems playing at the senior level, then the coach will move him down to the junior team for this season.

55. MICHAEL JOHNSON

55. MICHAEL JOHNSON

1. What happened to Michael three weeks ago?

2. Where is he studying now?

3. What is high school?

4. What is high school in some states in the U.S.?

5. Is Michael in a 3-year or a 4-year high school?

6. How does he compare to the other students in age?

7. What do most of the students seem like to Michael?

8. How many basketball teams does the school have?

9. Which team has Michael started practicing with?

10. What can you say about Michael's height?

11. How tall is he?

12. How many games did the high school coach see Michael play in last year?

13. Was Michael in high school or in middle school last year?

14. Did the coach see Michael in the state finals?

15. Describe Michael's performance in the state finals.

16. Why does the coach think Michael might be able to play on the senior team?

17. What does he think about Michael's future ability to play basketball when he's a little older?

18. Why does he think Michael could be one of the best in the nation?

19. Who is Dennis Fletcher?

20. Besides Dennis Fletcher, how many other boys are competing for the position of point guard?

21. How does Michael compare to two of the boys?

22. What is Dennis Fletcher's strongest point?

23. What was Dennis Fletcher's game point average last year?

24. Did he play on the junior team or on the senior team?

25. Where is Michael better than Dennis Fletcher?

26. What does Michael think the coach could do with Dennis Fletcher?

27. What decision has the coach made?

28. What will the coach do if Michael ends up having problems adapting?

ANSWERS

1. PHILIP JOHNSON

1. Phillip is 39 years old.
2. He's married.
3. Yes, he has children.
4. He has two children.
5. No, he doesn't live in New York.
6. He lives in Lincoln, Nebraska.
7. Yes, he lives in a nice house.
8. No, he isn't an actor.
9. He's the General Manager of a bank.
10. No, he doesn't work in a pharmacy.
11. He works in a bank.
12. No, it isn't outside of Lincoln.
13. The bank's in the center of Lincoln.
14. Yes, he has an important job.
15. He's the general manager.
16. Yes, he goes to work every day.
17. He goes to work at 8:30 in the morning.
18. No, he doesn't get there at 8:45.
19. He gets to the office at 9:00.
20. No, he doesn't park in the street.
21. He parks under the bank in the parking garage.
22. He works three and a half hours in the morning.
23. No, he doesn't spend a lot of time with customers.
24. He spends a lot of time talking on the telephone and reading reports.
25. No, he doesn't have lunch at home.
26. He usually has lunch at a restaurant near his office.
27. Yes, there are many good restaurants near his office.
28. He goes back to the office at 1:30 after lunch.
29. No, he doesn't stay there until 7:00.
30. He stays at the office until 6:00.
31. No, he doesn't go to a bar with his friends after work.
32. He usually goes home after work.
33. He usually gets home at 6:30.
34. No, he doesn't always go home after work.
35. Sometimes he goes to his son's school.
36. He goes there to watch him play basketball or baseball.
37. He gets home at 8:00 when he's with his son.
38. Yes, he likes his job.
39. He likes his job because he has a good salary and works with interesting people.
40. No, he doesn't travel very often in his job.
41. He needs to go to Omaha from time to time.
42. Omaha is 150 miles from Lincoln.
43. No, he doesn't usually stay for several days in Omaha.
44. He usually only stays for the day.
45. No, he doesn't always spend the night in Omaha.
46. No, he doesn't usually stay at the Palace Hotel.
47. He usually stays at the Omaha Sheraton Hotel.
48. Sometimes he stays in the Holiday Inn.
49. He prefers the Sheraton.
50. He prefers it because it has a breakfast buffet.

2. NANCY JOHNSON

1. No, Nancy isn't 33 years old.
2. Nancy is 38 years old.
3. No, she isn't Nigel's wife.
4. She's Phillip's wife.
5. She lives with her husband and children.
6. She lives in Lincoln.
7. No, she isn't from Nebraska.
8. She's from Kansas.
9. No, Kansas isn't far from Nebraska.
10. Yes, it's near Nebraska.
11. It's south of Nebraska.
12. No, she isn't a school teacher.
13. She's an interior decorator.
14. Yes, she teaches.
15. She teaches interior design.
16. No, she doesn't teach interior design in the evenings.
17. She teaches it in the mornings.
18. No, she doesn't teach it at a university.
19. She teaches it at a technical school.
20. No, the technical school isn't in the center of Lincoln.
21. It's 20 miles from Lincoln.
22. She teaches every day.
23. She starts her classes at 10:00.
24. She finishes at 12:00.
25. No, she doesn't have three classes.
26. She has two classes.
27. No, there aren't 20 students in each class.
28. There are about 15 students in each class.
29. No, she doesn't have lunch near the technical school.
30. She has lunch at home.
31. No, she doesn't stay at home after lunch.
32. She goes to her husband's bank after lunch.
33. No, she doesn't stay there all afternoon.
34. No, she doesn't spend an hour there.
35. She spends 30 minutes at the bank.
36. No, she doesn't spend the time with her husband.
37. She spends the time with a woman.
38. This woman is responsible for expansion.
39. Yes, she helps her.
40. She looks at plans for the new bank branches.
41. Yes, she gives recommendations.
42. She gives recommendations about the interior design and decoration.
43. No, she doesn't receive a nice salary for the help.
44. She doesn't receive any money.
45. No, she doesn't help the woman because she's bored.
46. She helps her because she's a good friend of hers.
47. She works as an independent decorator.
48. No, she doesn't work in an office.
49. She works at home when she isn't visiting clients.
50. She creates decoration plans or calls people.
51. No, she doesn't visit her clients every day.
52. She visits clients on some days.
53. No, she doesn't decorate only homes.
54. She decorates offices, restaurants and homes.
55. No, she doesn't like to decorate offices very much.
56. Because the companies usually prefer functional decoration and this is boring for her.
57. No, she doesn't like to decorate restaurants either.
58. Because often the owner of the restaurant thinks he's a professional decorator too.
59. Yes, she likes to decorate homes.
60. She likes to decorate homes because she is free to make more decisions and be more creative.

3. MICHAEL JOHNSON

1. No, he isn't 12 years old.
2. He's 14 years old.
3. No, he doesn't live alone.
4. He lives with his parents and sister.
5. No, he doesn't live in Kansas.
6. He lives in Lincoln, Nebraska.
7. No, he doesn't go to a private school.
8. He goes to a public school.
9. No, the school isn't far from his house.
10. It's near his house.
11. It's 10 minutes from his house by car.
12. No, his sister doesn't go to the same school.
13. She goes to a different school.
14. No, his school isn't far from his sister's school.
15. His school is 3 blocks from his sister's school.
16. Michael isn't in the eighth grade.
17. Michael is in the ninth grade.
18. No, he doesn't study just 3 subjects.
19. He studies six subjects.
20. Yes, he studies Speech and Music.
21. The other four subjects he studies are Math, Science, History and English.
22. Yes, he plays a musical instrument in music class.
23. No, he doesn't play the clarinet.
24. He plays the trumpet.
25. No, he isn't a member of the school band.
26. Because he doesn't have time to practice with the band after school.
27. No, the band doesn't practice before school.
28. The band practices after school.
29. No, school doesn't start at 9:30.
30. School starts at 9:00.
31. No, Michael doesn't often get to school late.
32. He gets to school early.
33. Because his father takes him.
34. His father takes him to school every day.
35. No, he doesn't leave him there at 8:30.
36. He leaves him there at 8:40.
37. No, he doesn't spend the 20 minutes studying.
38. He spends the time talking with his friends.
39. No, he doesn't have lunch at home.
40. He has lunch at school.
41. No, he doesn't have lunch at 12:30.
42. He has lunch at 12:00.
43. Yes, he usually eats a sandwich.
44. He also eats a bowl of soup.
45. No, he doesn't drink milk for lunch.
46. No, he doesn't drink Pepsi Cola.
47. He drinks a Coke.
48. No, his mother doesn't know that he drinks Coke.
49. She thinks he drinks milk.
50. Because Michael tells her that he drinks milk.
51. Yes, he has classes after lunch.
52. He finishes school at 3:30.
53. Yes, he likes sports.
54. He's a good athlete.
55. Yes, he plays sports at school
56. He plays three sports.
57. Yes, he plays basketball.
58. The other two sports he plays are football and baseball.
59. Yes, he's a member of the school team in them.
60. Yes, he's fast and strong.
61. He plays football in the fall.
62. He plays basketball in the winter.
63. He plays baseball in the spring.
64. Yes, he's a very popular boy at school.
65. He's popular because he's good at sports.
66. Yes, he's intelligent.
67. He isn't a good student.
68. He isn't a good student because he doesn't spend much time on his homework.
69. Yes, his teachers like him.
70. They tell his parents that

4. DENISE JOHNSON

1. Denise is 11 years old.
2. She lives with her parents and brother.
3. No, she doesn't live in Omaha.
4. She lives in Lincoln.
5. No, she doesn't attend a secondary school.
6. She attends a primary school.
7. No, she isn't in her first year.
8. She's in her last year.
9. No, she doesn't go to school by bus.
10. She goes to school with her father, who takes her every day with her brother.
11. No, she doesn't get to school a 9:00.
12. She gets to school at 8:45.
13. No, she doesn't study before class begins.
14. She goes to the playground.
15. No, she doesn't play with her brother in the playground.
16. She plays with her friends.
17. No, her first class doesn't begin at 8:45.
18. It begins at 9:00.
19. No, she's doesn't have 5 teachers during the morning.
20. She has the same teacher all morning. (She has one teacher all morning.)
21. No, she doesn't have this teacher all day.
22. She has the teacher all morning, until 12:00.
23. No, she doesn't have lunch 11:30.
24. She has lunch at 12:00.
25. No, she doesn't go home for lunch.
26. She has lunch in the school cafeteria.
27. No, she doesn't eat with her brother.
28. She eats with her two friends.
29. Yes, she always eats with the same friends.
30. Their names are Jenny and Pamela.
31. Yes, they spend a lot of time together.
32. They spend 9 or 10 hours together every day.
33. Yes, Denise's mother likes Jenny.
34. She doesn't like Pamela very much.
35. No, she doesn't think Pamela is introverted.
36. Becausse she thinks Pamela is very bossy.
37. No, she doesn't go home after school every day.
38. Sometimes she stays after school in the gym for ballet classes.
39. She stays after school two days a week.
40. She takes the ballet lessons in the gym.
41. No, she doesn't have a natural talent for ballet.
42. Yes, she likes to dance.
43. She has a very good technique.
44. She thinks that she has the potential to become a good dancer.
45. Denise finishes her ballet lessons at 4:30.
46. No, Pamela doesn't take ballet lessons.
47. Jenny takes ballet lessons with Denise.
48. No, Denise's mother doesn't take them home after the class.
49. No, she doesn't go home alone.
50. Jenny's mother takes her home.

5. NIGEL PERKINS

1. He's 55 years old.
2. No, he isn't American.
3. He's English.
4. No, he doesn't live in France.
5. He lives in England.
6. No, he doesn't live in London.
7. He lives north of London.
8. He lives 35 miles north of London.
9. He lives near the motorway.
10. He lives near the M-1 motorway.
11. He lives on a country estate.
12. He's married.
13. He's married to Margaret Perkins.
14. He has one child.
15. His son's name is Ronny.
16. Nigel owns a company.
17. It investigates people who receive big payments from insurance companies.
18. Yes, his company is famous.
19. Yes, it has many clients.
20. Yes, the majority of its clients are from the U.K.
21. It has some clients in France and in the U.S.
22. No, he doesn't go to the office every day.
23. He goes to the office two or three times a week.
24. No, it isn't near his estate.
25. It's in the center of London.
26. Yes, he has a good team of managers.
27. They run the company very well.
28. He reads and takes care of his garden.
29. Yes, it's big.
30. It covers almost 30,000 square meters.
31. Yes, he needs gardeners for his estate.
32. He needs three gardeners.
33. They work full-time.
34. No, he doesn't want to start a company in the U.S.
35. Yes, he wants to write.
36. He wants to write a book.
37. He wants to write a book about some of the interesting investigations from his company's past.
38. He thinks that they're good material for a novel or a suspense movie.
39. Ronny thinks he's crazy.
40. He doesn't pay any attention to Ronny.
41. No, he doesn't live with his parents.
42. He lives on the French Riviera.
43. No, he doesn't work in a bank.
44. He owns a small company.
45. The company rents yachts.
46. They go for short cruises between Monte Carlo and the Balearic Islands.
47. Yes, he makes a lot of money.
48. He makes it in the summer.
49. No, he doesn't make a lot of money in the winter.
50. He gets money from his father in the winter.

6. LUIGI BARGHINI

1. He's 49 years old.
2. He's from a small town.
3. It's in the north of Italy.
4. He lives outside Verona now.
5. He lives in a beautiful villa.
6. He lives with his wife.
7. His wife's name is Sofia.
8. He has a lot of money.
9. He has a lot of money because he owns a big factory.
10. It supplies car seats to Fiat.
11. It's in Turin.
12. He's the Chairman of the company.
13. His daughter Anna is the Managing Director.
14. She takes care of the day-to-day business of the company.
15. He spends a lot of time visiting different members of the Agnelli family.
16. He also spends time visiting Germany.
17. He visits Mercedes Benz in Germany.
18. He's negotiating a big contract to supply car seats to Mercedes Benz.
19. They're for small models.
20. It makes its small models in Stuttgart.
21. Yes, he's a very busy man.
22. He enjoys his work.
23. No, he doesn't stays at home when he isn't traveling.
24. He goes to the factory every day.
25. It's 23 kilometers away from his villa.
26. Yes, he sees his daughter when he goes there.
27. He visits the other workers.
28. He spends at least three hours with them.
29. He invites the workers to coffee.
30. He tells them jokes.
31. Yes, he likes them.
32. He enjoys human contact.
33. It's strong and healthy because he likes people and enjoys human contact.
34. He considers it a game.
35. Yes, he likes to win.
36. He has a good disposition.
37. No, he doesn't take things too seriously.
38. No, she isn't similar to him.
39. She's different because she's a manager, not an owner.

7. PIERRE MONET

1. He's 45 years old.
2. He lives in Paris.
3. He lives in the suburbs of Paris.
4. He's married.
5. He has three children.
6. Two of his children live at home.
7. He lives in a hall of residence not far from the Sorbonne.
8. It's near the Sorbonne.
9. He studies architecture.
10. No, he doesn't work in a company.
11. He's a civil servant.
12. He works in the Foreign Ministry.
13. He works in the translation and interpretation department.
14. It's in the center of Paris.
15. No, he doesn't drive to work every day.
16. He goes to work by train and subway.
17. No, it doesn't take him two hours to go to work.
18. It takes him almost an hour.
19. It takes him about 45 minutes to go back home.
20. He leaves at 7:00 in the morning.
21. He gets to the Ministry just before 8:00.
22. He has a lot of letters and documents waiting for him.
23. He's responsible for a special area.
24. He translates secret documents.
25. He speaks Spanish and English fluently.
26. He speaks Spanish fluently because his wife is Spanish.
27. He speaks English fluently because his mother is English.

28. Yes, he's an expert translator.
29. No, he doesn't usually translate documents in writing.
30. He verbally translates them directly into a microphone.
31. No, he doesn't transcribe the recordings.
32. A secretary transcribes the recordings.
33. Because this way he can translate very quickly and finish his work early.
34. No, he doesn't often finish work late.
35. He usually finishes early.
36. He usually goes home around 4:00 p.m.
37. No, he doesn't have lunch there.
38. Because he takes a sandwich to work every day.
39. He eats it at 12 o'clock sharp.
40. He prefers to work without interruptions in order to go home as early as possible.
41. He starts his second job.
42. He's a free lance translator.
43. He dictates his translations into his own microphone.
44. Her name is Anne-Marie.
45. She enters the recordings into a computer.
46. She does it the same evening, or the next morning.
47. She sends them by e-mail.
48. Pierre has a good salary at the Ministry.
49. He earns double at home.
50. He needs more money because his children all want to go to university.

8. PAULA EISENBACH

1. No, she isn't 40 years old.
2. She is 22 years old.
3. No, she doesn't live in Frankfurt.
4. She lives in Heidelberg.
5. No, she doesn't live there because she works there.
6. She lives in Heidelberg because she goes to the University of Heidelberg.
7. She's studying computer systems and graphic arts.
8. No, she isn't from Heidelberg.
9. She's from Munich.
10. Munich is in the south of Germany.
11. No, it isn't famous for its beer.
12. It's famous for its beauty and its university.
13. Yes, she likes it.
14. She lives in a flat.
15. No, she doesn't live alone.
16. She lives with two other friends.
17. One of them studies graphic arts.
18. No, the other friend isn't a student.
19. No, she isn't a fashion model.
20. She works in a fashion shop.
21. It's in the center of the town.
22. She spends all of her time attending classes, doing homework and helping Tom.
23. Tom is from the U.S.A.
24. Yes, he's a student.
25. No, he doesn't live outside of Heidelberg.
26. He lives near Paula in Heidelberg.
27. He's studying graphic arts.
28. He works part-time for the Walt Disney Corporation as an artist.
29. He draws cartoon characters and scenes for the Disney Corporation.
30. He receives instructions from the Disney people in California.
31. No, he doesn't receive the instructions by telephone.
32. He receives them over the Internet.
33. He sends them back to California by computer.
34. No, he doesn't do all the work alone.
35. Paula helps him.
36. She helps him in the evenings and sometimes on the weekends.
37. Yes, she likes it.
38. She likes it because she wants to improve her technique.
39. Yes, she's artistic.
40. No, she's doesn't like to spend a long time drawing.
41. Because she doesn't have the patience or discipline.
42. No, Tom isn't similar to her in this respect.
43. Yes, she's learning a lot from him.
44. They're very good friends.
45. Tom is from California.
46. He wants to go back for the Christmas holidays.
47. No, he doesn't want to go back alone.
48. He wants to invite Paula to go with him.
49. She's not sure if she wants to go.
50. The problem is that she doesn't know Tom very well yet.

9. LI TONG

1. No, he isn't 31 years old.
2. He's 36 years old.
3. No, he doesn't live in Peking.
4. He lives in Shanghai.
5. He lives in a small apartment.
6. No, he doesn't live with his mother.
7. He lives with his wife and young daughter.
8. Shanghai is a big city.
9. No, there aren't 20 million people in Shanghai.
10. There are 15 million people in Shanghai.
11. No, he doesn't work in an office.
12. He works in a factory.
13. No, the factory isn't near the mountains.
14. It's near the port.
15. No, the factory doesn't make shoes.
16. It makes telephones.
17. Yes, there's a big demand for telephones in China.
18. Li's apartment is very small.
19. No, it doesn't have three bedrooms.
20. It has one bedroom.
21. Li and his wife sleep in the bedroom.
22. Li's daughter sleeps in the living room.
23. Li's factory is doing very well.
24. His salary is increasing.
25. He has a television, a telephone and a washing machine.
26. No, his wife doesn't have a job.
27. Yes, she wants to work.
28. She's looking for a job.
29. She goes to a public school.
30. The school is near Li's house.
31. Li's daughter's grandfather takes her to school every day.
32. He gets to the house at 8:30 every morning.
33. He takes her home at 1 o'clock.
34. He takes her home at 1 o'clock for lunch.
35. He takes her back to school at 2:00.
36. No, she doesn't stay at school until 7:00 p.m.
37. She finishes school at 5:00 p.m.
38. He has lunch every day at Li's house.
39. He has lunch with his granddaughter.
40. No, he doesn't go to work by bus.
41. He goes to work by bicycle.
42. No, it doesn't take him 30 minutes to get to work.
43. It takes him almost an hour to get there.
44. He starts work at 6:00 a.m.
45. He finishes at 2:00 p.m.
46. He stays there for eight hours.
47. He gets home at 3:00.
48. No, he doesn't have lunch at home.
49. He has lunch at work.
50. No, he doesn't have lunch in the factory canteen.
51. His wife prepares his lunch for him.
52. She prepares it the night before.
53. She puts it in Li's shoulder bag.
54. He usually eats a chicken sandwich.
55. Because sometimes his wife doesn't have any chicken.
56. She prepares tofu when she doesn't have any chicken.
57. Tofu is a popular food made from soy beans.
58. He lives relatively well in comparison to other people.
59. No, he isn't a member of the lower class.
60. He's a member of the new middle class.

10. AKI MORITA

1. He's 39 years old.
2. No, he doesn't work for Toyota.
3. He works for Honda.
4. No, he isn't a factory worker.
5. Yes, he is an executive.
6. He's a young executive.
7. Yes, he's a member of a group of young executives.
8. They want to have an influence on the future of the company.
9. No, he isn't a lawyer.
10. He's an engineer.
11. No, he doesn't work in an engineering job.
12. He's the manager of the quality analysis department.
13. It counts all of the parts and components in the factory that have a defect.
14. No, there aren't many defects in them.
15. Because Aki and his people spend a lot of time visiting Honda's suppliers.
16. He gives them a quality manual.
17. He and his people spend 50% of their time with them.
18. He watches the process and finds ways to make it better.
19. It's probably responsible for the excellent quality record at Honda.
20. Yes, Aki's bosses know about his work.
21. Yes, he knows that they know.
22. He has a very good salary.
23. No, he doesn't live in Tokyo.
24. He lives in Osaka.
25. He lives in a nice area of Osaka.
26. Osaka is an industrial city.
27. Osaka is south of Tokyo.
28. He lives with his wife and two children.
29. No, he doesn't see them very often.
30. Because he works 14 hours every day and 5 or 6 hours on the weekend.
31. He works seventy-six hours every week.
32. No, he doesn't like to work so many hours.
33. No, he doesn't want to work less.
34. Because he thinks that it's the only way to move up in the organization.
35. No, he doesn't send them to a public school.
36. He sends them to a private school.
37. It's expensive.
38. No, she doesn't say anything about the hours he works.
39. She prefers the situation.
40. Because it gives her a lot of money to go shopping.

11. NATASHA ZARAKOVICH

1. She is 28 years old.
2. She lives with her mother and brother.
3. She lives in a small apartment.
4. No, she doesn't live in St. Petersburg.
5. She lives in Moscow.
6. No, she doesn't live near the Kremlin.
7. She lives near Gorky Park.
8. She is a chemist.
9. No, she doesn't work for a private company.
10. She works in the Russian State Laboratory.
11. It analyzes drugs that Russian laboratories produce.
12. Yes, it analyzes drugs from foreign companies.
13. Yes, she likes her job.
14. She has a good salary.
15. It's not far from her house.
16. No, she doesn't go to work by bus.
17. She goes to work on the subway.
18. It's only three stops from her house.
19. No, she doesn't read the newspaper on the subway.
20. She usually reads novels.
21. She reads novels in English.
22. Because she wants to improve her English.
23. Because she has a cousin in Scotland that she wants to visit.
24. Her cousin invites her to Scotland every year.
25. No, she doesn't go.
26. Because she doesn't have enough money to go.
27. Yes, she wants to go.
28. She wants to go next year.
29. She starts work at 7:30 in the morning.
30. Yes, she prefers to go to work early.
31. Because there are fewer people in the subway at that time.
32. She doesn't take any breaks during the morning.
33. No, she doesn't have lunch in the laboratory.
34. She has lunch at home.
35. She goes home for lunch at 12:00.
36. She has lunch with her mother.
37. She gets back to the lab at 1:30.
38. She finishes work at 4:30.
39. No, she doesn't always leave at 4:30.
40. She sometimes stays later if her boss needs her help.
41. She usually goes to the national library.
42. It's near the laboratory.
43. She stays until 6:30 or 7:00.
44. No, she doesn't like to go home to read and study.
45. Because her house is small and noisy.
46. It's partuculary noisy when her brother and his friends are there.
47. She likes the library because it's quiet.
48. She reads in English.
49. She wants to take the State English Examination.
50. If she passes it, she will automatically receive an increase in her salary.

12. INÉS GARCÍA

1. Inés is 24 years old.
2. She lives with her parents.
3. She lives in the south of Spain.
4. She lives in Seville.
5. She lives outside of Seville.
6. She lives 20 kilometers from Seville.
7. She lives 20 kilometers east of Seville.
8. No, she isn't a doctor.
9. She is a lawyer.
10. No she doesn't work in the public sector.
11. Yes, she works in a law firm.
12. She works in her father's law firm.
13. This is her first year in the firm.
14. Yes, she does a lot of different things in the firm.
15. She does a lot of the jobs that the other lawyers don't like to do.
16. They ask her for help because she knows how to use computers well.
17. No, she doesn't mind helping them.
18. She gets the impression they are taking advantage of her.
19. She works on legal cases that other lawyers don't want to handle.
20. She spends a lot of time at the court defending cases.
21. She defends labor cases.
22. Her father's firm has a lot of big companies as clients.

23. She spends time preparing cases concerning labor disputes.
24. Her father says that it's good experience.
25. Yes, she agrees with him.
26. She prepares them very well.
27. No, she doesn't want to work with labor cases for long.
28. In the future, she wants to work in mergers and acquisitions.
29. An acquisition is where one company buys another company.
30. A merger is where two companies join to create a new one.
31. She likes it because it includes a lot of financial aspects.
32. Yes, she is taking a special course now.
33. She's taking a course in business management and finance.
34. She attends the class at the University of Seville.
35. The class takes place at night.
36. No, she doesn't go there every night.
37. She goes there three nights a week.
38. The class lasts three hours.
39. It begins at 6:00 p.m.
40. It ends at 9:00 p.m.

13. PHILLIP JOHNSON

1. Yes, he had a busy morning yesterday.
2. No, he didn't get up at the usual time.
3. He got up at 7:00.
4. He usually gets up at 7:30.
5. Because his wife had to leave home very early.
6. Nancy had to leave home early to take a report to a client.
7. The client was 70 miles from Lincoln.
8. She left home at 7:25.
9. Phillip made breakfast for himself.
10. Nancy usually makes breakfast.
11. Yes, it was an exception.
12. Phillip took a shower and had breakfast before they got up.
13. He prepared fried eggs and toast for them.
14. He left home at 8:30.
15. No, he didn't leave alone.
16. He left home with his children.
17. Because he took them to school.
18. He got to the office at ten minutes past nine.
19. Yes, he had meetings during the morning.
20. He had three meetings.
21. No, the first one wasn't at 9:30.
22. It was at 10 o'clock.
23. No, it wasn't with a salesman.
24. It was with the bank's lawyer.
25. Yes, they discussed a problem.
26. An important client wanted to suspend payments on a loan.
27. No, they didn't make a final decision during the meeting.
28. They decided to wait until the meeting of the bank's Board of Directors to make a final decision.
29. The second meeting was at 11:30.
30. He received the owner of a ceramic factory near Lincoln.
31. The man needed 500,000 dollars.
32. He needed it to add a new building to his factory.
33. It was one of the best in Nebraska.
34. He knew the man very well and trusted him.
35. He met with the chief commercial officer of the bank.
36. They discussed a salary question concerning one of the employees.
37. It lasted thirty minutes.
38. He went to lunch at 12:30.
39. He had lunch with the chief commercial officer.
40. They had lunch in a small restaurant near the office.

14. NANCY JOHNSON

1. No, she didn't have a normal morning yesterday.
2. She usually gets up at 7:30.
3. She got up at 6:30 yesterday.
4. She took a shower and got dressed.
5. She left home at 7:25.
6. She had to drive 70 miles to Mr. Evans's house.
7. The house is west of Lincoln.
8. She had to deliver an interior design plan.
9. He's the owner of a house she's decorating.
10. He's building a new master bedroom.
11. It's for him and his wife.
12. He needed to give the plan to the company that is building the bedroom.
13. Because she didn't have any time the rest of the day to drive to Mr. Evans's house.
14. She had to be at the technical school at 10 o'clock.
15. The technical school is 20 miles east of Lincoln.

16. It's 90 miles from Mr. Evans's house.
17. Because she had to drive to Mr. Evans' house and then drive to the technical school.
18. Because she teaches an interior design class at 10:00.
19. She drove relatively fast.
20. She got to his house at 8:35.
21. She spent ten minutes talking to him.
22. She talked to him about some details of the plan.
23. She left his house at 8:45.
24. The trip was an hour and ten minutes long.
25. No, there wasn't a lot of traffic.
26. Because Lincoln is a relatively small city.
27. She got to the school at exactly five minutes to ten.
28. She had a quick coffee before going to her class.
29. She had a coffee with one of the other teachers.
30. She entered her class at two minutes past ten.

15. NIGEL PERKINS

1. He flew to Monte Carlo last week.
2. He went with his wife.
3. They went there to visit their son.
4. They fly to Monte Carlo two or three times every year.
5. They go there between November and March.
6. Because their son Ronny is too busy the other half of the year.
7. They left from Gatwick Airport.
8. They drove to the airport.
9. They flew to Monte Carlo on Wednesday.
10. They left their car at the airport parking lot.
11. They had first class reservations on the flight.
12. The plane left on time.
13. It left at 11:15.
14. It got to Monte Carlo early.
15. It arrived at five minutes past one.
16. Nobody met them at the airport.
17. No, they weren't expecting to meet Ronny at the airport.
18. They caught a taxi.
19. They went to Ronny's apartment.
20. The apartment is near the port.
21. No, he wasn't at home when they got there.
22. They were surprised.
23. No, they didn't go up to the apartment.
24. Because they didn't have a key.
25. They spent some time looking at the shop windows along the street.
26. They spent 20 minutes looking at the shops.
27. They went back to the apartment building.
28. No, he wasn't there.
29. It was cold.
30. She felt a little cold.
31. They decided to go to a small book-shop near the apartment.
32. It was about 300 meters from Ronny's apartment.
33. Nigel likes bookshops but Margaret doesn't.
34. He asked permission to use the telephone.
35. He called Ronny's mobile number.
36. Ronny was in a meeting.
37. He was in a meeting with a tour operator.
38. He told Nigel that the porter had a key to his apartment.
39. They walked back to the building, called the porter, and asked for the key.
40. Ronny got home two hours later.

16. NATASHA ZARAKOVICH

1. She had a big surprise.

2. Yesterday was her birthday.

3. She thought nobody at the lab knew it was her birthday.

4. No, she didn't want to tell them.

5. Because Russian people always bring a lot of food to the office to celebrate a birthday.

6. Because she was on a strict diet.

7. She didn't remember that Gregori was going out a lot with one of her best friends.

8. They had lunch together.

9. She told him that it was Natasha's birthday.

10. She was planning to go to the library at 4:30.

11. He called her at 4:20.

12. He asked her to help him with a report.

13. He said he wanted to finish it before 5:30.

14. She thought this was strange.

15. Because Gregori doesn't usually ask her to work late.

16. She went to his office.

17. It's on the third floor.

18. There were ten people there when she got there.

19. They were waiting for her.

20. They wanted to celebrate her birthday.

21. They had cakes and tea waiting for her.

22. They stayed in the office until 7:00 p.m.

23. Yes, they had a good time.

24. He invited all of them to a nightclub.

25. It was in the center of Moscow.

26. There was good vodka at the club.

27. They played folk music.

28. They ate, drank and danced there.

29. They left at 10:30.

30. She got home at 11:00.

31. She talked to her mother.

32. She talked to her for a few minutes.

33. She had to get up early this morning.

34. She was glad that today was Friday.

17. AKI MORITA

1. He had the meeting last Friday.
2. There were two other people in the meeting.
3. He had the meeting with his boss and his boss's boss.
4. Yes, he knew about the meeting in advance.
5. Yes, he thought he knew the subject of the meeting.
6. He thought it was going to be about a new supplier.
7. The meeting was in a meeting room.
8. His boss offered him a coffee.
9. He said the meeting was about Louisiana.
10. He didn't understand.
11. He remembered that Honda was building a new factory in the United States.
12. The factory was going to be in a city called Baton Rouge.
13. No, he wasn't nervous.
14. No, he didn't understand the reason for the meeting at first.
15. He told him that Honda wanted a good man to go to Louisiana.
16. They wanted to organize a quality department.
17. Yes, they wanted to establish the same quality system in the United States.
18. Yes, the system was successful in Japan.
19. He immediately thought about his family.
20. He asked his boss about the duration of the stay in Louisiana.
21. The stay in Louisiana was for three years or maybe more.
22. Aki speaks English well.
23. His wife doesn't speak English well.
24. His children are young.
25. They have English classes every day at school.
26. No, they don't take the classes at home.
27. They take them at school.
28. No, he didn't accept the offer during the meeting.
29. He told them that he wanted to discuss the matter with his family.
30. They said that they needed an answer by next week.
31. No, he didn't visit a supplier after the meeting.
32. He went home after the meeting.
33. He got home at 9:30.
34. Yes, his wife was at home when he got there.
35. She was busy helping the children with their homework.
36. No, he didn't tell her about the meeting.
37. He decided to tell her the next day.
38. He considered the situation an order.
39. No, the next day wasn't Tuesday.
40. The next day was Saturday.

18. PIERRE MONET

1. Pierre considers himself an artist.
2. Yes, he considers translating a difficult job.
3. He was going to meet the Prime Minister of France.
4. The Prime Minister wanted to congratulate Pierre.
5. He wanted to congratulate him for a job well done.
6. He considered it as simply another translation job.
7. He did a special job this time.
8. He received the document last Tuesday.
9. It was a speech.
10. It was in French.
11. He was going to speak to the British Parliament.
12. He was going to use English in the speech.
13. The instructions were simple.
14. He knew that the Prime Minister didn't speak English well.
15. He made the decision to translate the speech into simple, direct English.
16. His style was to write speeches in complicated French.
17. Pierre decided to change the style of the speech.
18. He had to maintain the power of the message.
19. He started on the translation at 9:30 in the morning.
20. He finished it just before 3:00 p.m.
21. His boss sent the translation to the Prime Minister.
22. He sent it by special e-mail.
23. His boss received a phone call from the Prime Minister.
24. He received it two days later.
25. The Prime Minister invited Pierre and his boss to his office.
26. He invited them to a coffee.
27. He invited them for the next day.
28. Yes, he read the speech.
29. He was surprised at first.
30. Yes, he continued reading it.
31. He thought that the message was perfectly expressed.
32. He thought Pierre's version was more effective and powerful than the original.
33. Pierre's boss congratulated Pierre.
34. He was excited because of the opportunity to have a coffee with the Prime Minister.

19. DENISE JOHNSON

1. She was nervous last Monday.
2. She was in her ballet class when she became nervous.
3. The class was after school.
4. She was with the other students.
5. She told them a woman was coming.
6. The woman was from the American Academy of Dance.
7. She was going to give them an examination.
8. She was going to give it on Thursday.
9. The exam was held every year.
10. No, not all the girls had to take the exam.
11. The girls who wanted to continue with ballet at the Academy had to take it.
12. This was the first exam.
13. They became members of the Academy.
14. They started in the category of elementary one.
15. The teacher told them to tell their parents that the exam cost 15 dollars and the membership 10 dollars a year.
16. No, she didn't want to take it.
17. Because she always got very nervous when she had to take a test or an exam.
18. She told her mother about it that night.
19. No, she didn't want to become a member of the Academy.
20. Because she didn't like to take exams.
21. She thought that Denise had a lot of potential.
22. She told her she had good technique.
23. She told her that the exam was probably very easy.
24. No, this didn't convince Denise to take the exam.
25. She took her to the best shop in Lincoln for ballet shoes.
26. She took her to the shop the next day.
27. They bought a pair of beautiful shoes and other things.
28. Denise liked the shoes very much.
29. She decided to take the exam.
30. She knew that Denise only needed a little persuasion.

20. LUIGI BARGHINI

1. He went to Germany last week.
2. He stayed there for three days.
3. He flew to Stuttgart.
4. No, he didn't go there alone.
5. He flew there with his daughter, Anna.
6. They stayed at the Regency Hotel.
7. No, they didn't have three meetings on the fist day.
8. They had one meeting on the first day.
9. They had the meeting with the Chairman of Mercedes Benz.
10. No, they didn't talk about a possible contract.
11. They talked about the Agnelli family.
12. They had lunch with the Chairman and with the Managing Director of Mercedes Benz.
13. No, they didn't have lunch in a local restaurant.
14. They had lunch in the private dining room on the top floor.
15. They talked about the market situation for luxury cars and about the competition from Japanese car makers.
16. No, they didn't stay at Mercedes after lunch.
17. They went back to the hotel after lunch.
18. They spent two hours planning meetings for the next day.
19. They had three meetings for the next day.
20. They had dinner with the Purchasing Manager of Mercedes.
21. Yes, Karl knew Anna very well.
22. Because the two companies were negotiating a contract for car seats.
23. Karl was 34 years old.
24. He was single.
25. He wanted to work with Luigi's company because he wanted to continue seeing Anna as much as possible.
26. Because she was beautiful and rich.
27. He didn't know if she was having a relationship with anyone in Italy.
28. He noticed that Karl was paying a lot of attention to Anna.
29. No, he didn't say anything to her about it.
30. Because he wanted to concentrate on the important meetings for the next day.

21. LI TONG

1. He decided to learn English.
2. He made the decision at exactly 11:15 in the morning.
3. He was working in the telephone factory.
4. He saw a young man at 11:00.
5. The man was Chinese.
6. He was with two men.
7. The men were tall.
8. He saw that they were wearing ties.
9. No, they didn't appear to be Japanese.
10. They appeared to be English or American.
11. The young man was Speaking English.
12. He was explaining the production process.
13. The young man asked Li a few questions about his job.
14. Li told him he was responsible for inserting the microphone in the telephone receiver.
15. Yes, he translated what Li said.
16. They looked at the work and smiled at Li.
17. Yes, they said something to him.
18. They spoke to him in English.
19. Li answered them in Chinese.
20. Li thought they said "thank you".
21. He said "thank you" to them in Chinese.
22. They left and continued walking around the factory.
23. Li went back to his work.
24. He thought about the young Chinese employee.
25. He was sure that the young man probably earned a lot more money than he did.
26. He knew that the company was growing very fast.
27. Some of them were now working in office jobs.
28. They were earning more than Li.
29. He decided to learn English.
30. He didn't know how much it cost to take classes.
31. He decided to ask one of his friends.
32. He worked in the same department as the young man.
33. Li knew that his friend was going to a language school.
34. It was less than 500 meters from where Li lived.

22. INÉS GARCÍA

1. She had a traffic accident.
2. No, it didn't happen in the morning.
3. It happened at about 5:45 p.m.
4. She was going to the University of Seville.
5. She was going there for her evening course in Business Management and Finance.
6. It was Inés' fault.
7. She was driving a Ford Puma.
8. She was driving through the center of Seville.
9. The streets are narrow in that area.
10. She was talking on her mobile phone.
11. She was talking to Paco, her boyfriend.
12. She didn't notice a stop sign in front of her.
13. She ran the stop sign.
14. Another car hit her.
15. It hit her on the passenger side.
16. It was a small car.
17. It was an Opel Corsa.
18. It wasn't a serious accident.
19. Because both of the cars in the accident were small.
20. She cut her phone conversation.
21. She got out of her car.
22. She went to the other car.
23. She went to it to speak to the driver.
24. Because she saw that he was a young man.
25. He was probably the same age as her.
26. Yes, he smiled when he got out of his car.
27. He said hello.
28. He said hello in Spanish.
29. He had a French accent.
30. She looked at him and didn't say anything.
31. He was tall and very attractive.
32. He seemed like a very pleasant person.
33. She usually talks a lot.
34. No, she didn't talk a lot this time.
35. Because she didn't know what to say.
36. He asked her if she had her car papers.
37. She went back to her car.
38. She got the papers.
39. It took them less than ten minutes to finish it.
40. His name was François Monet.
41. He invited her to have a coffee with him.
42. The coffee shop was across the street.
43. Inés accepted the invitation.
44. She disconnected her mobile telephone.

23. MICHAEL JOHNSON

1. He was the star of his basketball team.
2. They were playing in the regional finals.
3. His team won easily.
4. The final score was 67 to 42.
5. The other team was the favorite to win the game.
6. Michael set two records.
7. He set a team record and also a record for the state of Nebraska.
8. He scored more than 30 points.
9. He scored 41 points.
10. He scored more points in the second half.
11. He scored 16 points in the first half.
12. He scored 25 points in the second half.
13. Yes, there was a press photographer there.
14. His picture was in the newspaper the next day.
15. Michael made seven baskets in the first three minutes of the second half.
16. Only two of his points were free throws.
17. Yes, he read the article.
18. He started to receive phone calls from them.
19. Yes, he received a call from a basketball coach.
20. The coach was from the high school that Michael was going to attend next year.
21. The coach was going to watch the next game.
22. No, the next game wasn't against another Lincoln school.
23. It was against the Omaha Buffaloes.
24. He told him that the Buffaloes were the best basketball team in Nebraska at middle school level.
25. No, he wasn't worried about them.
26. He knew that the Buffaloes weren't a good defensive team.
27. He planned to play the same way as in the last game.
28. He was sure that his team was going to win.
29. His father agreed with him.
30. She told him that he needed to concentrate more on his studies and less on basketball.

24. PAULA EISENBACH

1. She spent last Tuesday with Tom Sanders.
2. She spent the afternoon with him.
3. She worked with him for about 10 hours a week.
4. No, she didn't help him with his studies.
5. She helped him with his drawings for the Disney Corporation.
6. Tom worked with Disney.
7. He had a contract to draw cartoons for Disney animated movies.
8. She thought he was an excellent artist.
9. Yes, she liked working with him.
10. Because she learned a lot about drawing technique.
11. Tom paid her $15 an hour.
12. He paid her in dollars.
13. Because the Disney Corporation paid him in dollars.
14. He told her that he wanted to take her to California to meet his parents.
15. No, it wasn't a surprise for her.
16. Yes, she knew that Tom wanted her to go with him.
17. She wasn't sure she wanted to go.
18. Yes, she liked Tom as a person.
19. She wasn't sure about her feelings for him.
20. She considered him to be a wonderful person.
21. She felt she wasn't ready to expand her relationship with him.
22. She didn't understand his reason for inviting her to California.
23. They were only friends.
24. She called her parents.
25. They lived in Munich.
26. She told them about the situation with Tom.
27. Her father told her that she had to make the decision herself.
28. Her mother told her that it wasn't a good idea.
29. She said it was dangerous for her to go to California if she didn't feel anything special for Tom.
30. Paula decided to think about it for a few days before giving Tom a final answer.

25. NIGEL PERKINS

---

1. No, it hasn't been an easy week for Nigel.

2. This has been a busy one for him.

3. He has had to work more than usual.

4. His company has discovered some very important evidence.

5. An insurance company contacted his firm.

6. They contacted his firm two months ago.

7. They wanted his firm to investigate an unusual case.

8. He was 62 years old.

9. He was married when he died.

10. No, she wasn't the same age as him.

11. She was 32 years old when he died.

12. She was a model before she got married.

13. She received seven million dollars.

14. She received it from the insurance company.

15. He died of a heart attack.

16. Yes, Nigel's company investigated his death.

17. Yes, the insurance company suspected something.

18. Yes, Nigel's company found something suspicious.

19. They discovered that the woman had bought medicine.

20. She bought a large amount of this medicine.

21. People who suffer from hemophilia usually buy it.

22. It's the worst kind for people who have bad blood circulation.

23. He probably didn't suffer from hemophilia.

24. Yes, he probably had a circulation problem.

25. Yes, he knew the man personally.

26. He was a good friend of the man's.

27. Yes, he personally helped in the investigation.

28. Because he felt it was his obligation.

26. INÉS GARCÍA

1. No, she hasn't had an easy day today.
2. She has had a difficult day.
3. No, she hasn't attended three meetings today.
4. She has attended two meetings.
5. Yes, she has gone to the courthouse today.
6. She has gone there twice.
7. She has defended two different cases.
8. She has defended labor cases.
9. She has given a lecture on labor law.
10. She has done these things in a period of 8 hours.
11. She hasn't had time to do three other things that need her attention.
12. She hasn't had time to buy him a birthday present yet.
13. His birthday is the day after tomorrow.
14. She hasn't had time to make an appointment.
15. Yes, she needs to go to the dentist.
16. She needs to repair a crown that broke yesterday.
17. She hasn't talked to François Monet.
18. He's the young man from Paris whom she met in the car accident.
19. It was two weeks ago.
20. He left a message on her mobile phone.
21. Because she was in one of the meetings in the law firm.
22. She has tried to return the call three times.
23. Because his line has been busy.
24. It has been busy all day.
25. Yes, she has spoken to him since the accident.
26. She has spoken to him twice.
27. Yes, he has invited her to Paris.
28. Yes, she has been to Paris.
29. She went to Paris when she was 11 years old.
30. She spent three days there.
31. She hasn't been back since then.
32. She has been thinking a lot about François.
33. She has made the decision to start learning French.
34. She hasn't told her boyfriend about him yet.

27. NATASHA ZARAKOVICH

1. She has been thinking about Scotland.
2. She has been thinking about it for the past two weeks.
3. His name is André Zarakovich.
4. He has been living there for 23 years.
5. He moved there with his parents.
6. He was five years old when he moved there.
7. He is one year younger than Natasha.
8. He lived in Moscow.
9. He lived near Natasha.
10. They played together.
11. He only remembers a few things.
12. She remembers a lot of things.
13. He was a bad little boy.
14. He hit her when they were playing.
15. They have been writing to each other for the past five years.
16. He's an aeronautical engineer.
17. They have a nice house in Glasgow.
18. They live in the suburbs of Glasgow.
19. Since he started writing to her five years ago.
20. Yes, she would like to go.
21. The problem is that it's too expensive for her.
22. He told her that he had found a new job and is earning more money.
23. He's earning twice as much in his new job.
24. He made a flight reservation for her.
25. He made it with British Airways.
26. She'll go to Scotland on December 22nd.
27. No, she won't stay for several months.
28. She'll go back to Moscow on January 3rd.
29. She couldn't believe it.
30. She didn't like the idea of André paying for the ticket.
31. She was excited because she was finally going to visit another country.
32. She has never traveled abroad.
33. She has never been to St. Petersburg.
34. No, she has never been to another large city in Russia.
35. Yes, she has been outside of Moscow.
36. She has been 50 kilometers outside of Moscow.

28. ANNA BARGHINI

1. She received a telephone call from Karl Polster.

2. She received it shortly before lunch.

3. Karl is the Purchasing Manager.

4. They've been in contact for several months.

5. Because Anna's company is negotiating a large contract to supply car seats for Mercedes.

6. She's having lunch right now.

7. She's thinking about Karl.

8. It seems strange that he calls her so often.

9. Karl's job is more administrative than technical.

10. The negotiations are more technical than administrative.

11. They're dealing with the technical people at Mercedes.

12. Anna has a feeling that he's interested in more than business with her.

13. He asked her when she was planning to visit Stuttgart again.

14. He also talked about his country house in the Black Forest.

15. She doesn't have a serious relationship with any man right now.

16. She's too busy right now to worry about men.

17. She's 27 years old.

18. Sometimes she feels a little lonely.

19. She thinks he's a nice young man and quite handsome.

20. She's afraid that men are more interested in her money than in her.

21. It's worth over 50 million dollars.

22. She told him she was planning to be there for a couple of days.

23. She said she would be there at the end of November.

24. She didn't say anything when he mentioned it.

29. AKI MORITA

1. He was worried about his future in Honda.

2. They had told him that he would be the quality manager at a new factory Honda was building in Louisiana.

3. No, he didn't tell them about Louisiana when he got home.

4. He got out his encyclopedia when he got home.

5. He looked up "Louisiana" in his encyclopedia.

6. It said that it was famous for its French influence.

7. It talked about a group of French Protestants called "Acadians".

8. They had gone to Louisiana to escape persecution.

9. They had established a special culture called "Cajun".

10. It's called "Cajun" because it is a deformation of the word "Acadian".

11. It mentioned the city of New Orleans.

12. He read about the history of Louisiana.

13. He read about the political corruption in the state during the '30's and '40's.

14. He found the section about the plantation homes interesting.

15. They were located along the Mississippi River in a town called Natchez.

16. He thought his wife would enjoy visiting Natchez.

17. He sat down to have dinner after he had finished reading.

18. He had dinner with his family.

19. He sat down at 8:30 to have dinner.

20. She noticed that he was quiet.

21. She didn't say anything about it.

22. She thought he had had a hard day at the office.

23. No, he wasn't usually fun and talkative when he was at home.

24. He was often quiet and pensive at home.

30. PIERRE MONET

1. He had a terrible time getting up.
2. He had an important translation to do at the Ministry.
3. He would have stayed in bed until at least 10 o'clock.
4. He had gone to bed at 4:00 a.m.
5. He had spent 10 hours doing it.
6. He did the translation for a personal client.
7. The client needed it by 8 o'clock that very morning.
8. No, he didn't know about it when he got home the day before.
9. No, he didn't start doing it when he got home.
10. He began working on a short, easy translation about a corporate merger.
11. It needed to be finished by the following Monday.
12. He received a phone call from the Chairman of Peugeot.
13. He received the call at 5:30.
14. Yes, he knew Pierre personally.
15. Because he had used his services before.
16. He had a meeting with the management of Volvo.
17. It's located in Sweden.
18. It was originally scheduled for the following week.
19. The meeting had been moved up to tomorrow.
20. He needed Pierre to translate two letters and a 24-page contract.
21. This would mean staying up all night.
22. He told him not to worry.
23. He received the documents within five minutes.
24. He received them by e-mail.
25. By 7:00 p.m., he had finished the two letters.
26. One of them was four pages long.
27. She made him a sandwich and a strong coffee.
28. He had already finished the first six pages of the contract by that time.
29. It was quite difficult to translate.
30. It included a lot of legal terminology and very long sentences.
31. It was so long that it took Pierre almost a minute to find the subject and the verb.
32. By 3:00 a.m., he had finished the contract.
33. He checked the contract thoroughly.
34. He sent it to Peugeot shortly before 4:00 a.m.
35. He sent it to them by e-mail.
36. He felt exhausted.
37. His only consolation was that he would earn almost 1,000 euros for the job.
38. He felt that his effort was worth it.

31. FRANÇOIS MONET

1. He's Pierre Monet's nephew.
2. He's 27 years old.
3. No, he doesn't work in a Spanish company.
4. He works in a French chemical company.
5. He's a salesman.
6. He travels to many factories throughout the E.U.
7. He goes to Huelva when he travels to Spain.
8. He rents a car when he's in Spain.
9. He met her in a traffic accident
10. Because otherwise he wouldn't have met Inés.
11. He thinks about her every day.
12. He calls her as often as he can.
13. He has invited her to visit Paris.
14. He's a little afraid of having a more serious relationship.
15. Because he doesn't understand the character of the people from the south of Spain, especially from Seville.
16. They seem like fun people who look for ways to enjoy life.
17. He saw the opera "Carmen" several years ago.
18. The soldier fell in love with a gypsy girl from Seville.
19. He had all kinds of problems.
20. No, she isn't a gypsy.
21. He remembers her black hair and dark eyes.
22. She had black hair and dark eyes too.
23. François finds her very attractive.
24. He thought she was very different from the girls in Paris.
25. He invited her to visit Paris.
26. He has called her three times since then.
27. Because her mobile phone was disconnected each time.
28. He hopes she'll call him.

32. LI TONG

1. No, he hasn't just finished work.
2. He has just finished his first English class.
3. He's going home now.
4. It's about a kilometer from his house.
5. It took him about 10 minutes to get there.
6. He went there on his bike.
7. He was sent to room 11.
8. There were seven other students there when he got there.
9. They were waiting for the teacher to arrive.
10. He sat at the back of the room.
11. He sat next to a large window.
12. He could see a lot of people coming and going through the window.
13. Most of the people were using bicycles.
14. The teacher came into the room.
15. He was carrying a lot of books.
16. He put them on a small desk.
17. It was in front of the class.
18. He wrote his name on the board.
19. No, he didn't understand what the teacher wrote.
20. Because he didn't know the English or Latin alphabet.
21. It looked like strange symbols.
22. Because he said something.
23. He assumed the teacher was saying his name.
24. It sounded like he was saying "pita".
25. He pointed at different students.
26. He just looked at the teacher without saying anything.
27. He whispered something to the first student.
28. He responded by saying his name, 'Han".
29. He made the first student say some strange sounds finishing with the name "Han".
30. He felt a little nervous.
31. Because he knew the teacher was going to ask him the same question.
32. He listened carefully to them.
33. He repeated the sounds, finishing with "Li".
34. He seemed satisfied.
35. He went back to the blackboard.
36. He realized that he had just said his first sentence in English.

33. LUIGI BARGHINI

1. He has just finished his engineering degree.
2. No, he didn't study engineering in the U.K.
3. He studied engineering at the University of Milan.
4. He's proud because he graduated second in his class.
5. It took him six years to get his degree.
6. It usually takes five years to get a degree.
7. Because he specialized in two different fields of industrial engineering.
8. He specialized in organization and robotics.
9. It's rare because it's usually not permitted.
10. He asked his father to speak to the Dean of the Engineering School at the university to get permission.
11. He thought that his son was a little crazy to want to study two different areas.
12. Yes, he helped him get permission.
13. He was able to help him because the Dean knew Luigi quite well.
14. Because the Dean had been one year ahead of him at the same university.
15. They studied together 30 years ago.
16. The Dean is older.
17. No, they weren't close friends at that time.
18. He had stayed in contact with him because he had asked him to send him the best young engineers graduating from the University of Milan.
19. They had helped Luigi's company become the second largest car seat manufacturer in Europe.
20. He has to make a decision about Roberto.
21. He has just turned 24.
22. He would like to work as a consultant in organization and computer integrated systems.
23. Luigi thinks he should work in the family company.
24. He has received an offer from accenture.
25. Their headquarters are in the U.S.
26. They're in Milan.
27. He is tempted to take the job.
28. He thinks Anna is perfectly capable of running the family business with Luigi's help.
29. He doesn't see much challenge in working in a car seat factory.
30. He thinks that they could easily become the number one supplier of car seats in Europe.

34. PAULA EISENBACH

1. She feels relieved today.
2. She spoke to her friend, Tom Sanders.
3. She told him that she had decided not to go to California with him.
4. No, he wasn't relieved.
5. He was very upset.
6. They argued.
7. She finally told him the truth.
8. She said that she enjoyed working with him and that she had learned a lot, but that she wasn't ready to have a deeper relationship.
9. He told her that he didn't want her to help him anymore with the Disney drawings.
10. No, it wasn't a surprise for her. She knew he would react that way.
11. She had been helping him for almost two months.
12. She had become convinced he wasn't a stable person.
13. He was a brilliant artist in her opinion.
14. He was very introverted.
15. His problem was that he didn't know how to respond to people in a natural way.
16. She called her parents in Munich.
17. She told them her decision.
18. She was relieved.
19. He told her that she had made the right decision.
20. They told her they were thinking about spending a week in the Canary Islands during the Christmas holidays.
21. They asked her if she would like to go.
22. She jumped at the opportunity.
23. She was tired of the cold weather in Heidelberg.
24. She felt it would be the perfect remedy.

35. NANCY JOHNSON

1. Yes, she has a problem.
2. It's a pleasant problem.
3. She and her family would be rich by now.
4. She has been offered a job to decorate the home that George Clooney owns.
5. It's in Aspen, Colorado.
6. It's the most famous ski resort in the United States.
7. She'll discuss the problem with her husband, Phillip.
8. She'll call Eddie Campbell.
9. He is a famous interior decorator and the most prestigious professor of interior design in California.
10. He teaches it at U.C.L.A.
11. It stands for the University of California at Los Angeles.
12. He does other things.
13. He helps the Hollywood rich to decorate their homes in Beverly Hills and Malibu Beach.
14. His students help him.
15. They have them in Beverly Hills.
16. Yes, he knows Nancy very well.
17. Because they studied interior design together.
18. They studied it at the University of Kansas.
19. He knew Eddie personally because Eddie and his students decorated his home in Beverly Hills.
20. They decorated it seven years ago.
21. He called Eddie last week.
22. He called to ask him to decorate his new home in Colorado.
23. He told him he couldn't do it, but that he had the perfect person for the job.
24. Nancy's mother and sister live in Coffeyville.
25. Her sister is single.
26. Nancy thinks they could come up to Lincoln from time to time to stay with the kids.
27. Nancy could have time to go to Colorado and do the job.
28. She thinks the technical school would give her the time off from work.
29. Because it would mean a lot for the school to have a teacher who's decorating the home of George Clooney.
30. She wonders what Phillip will say about it.

36. DENISE JOHNSON

1. She had a fight with Pamela Stanley.
2. It happened last Friday afternoon.
3. It happened in the backyard of another friend, Jenny.
4. She lives on the same block as the other two.
5. They were playing a guessing game.
6. The rules were simple.
7. The leader had to think of someone famous.
8. They had to guess who the other person was by asking questions.
9. They had to ask "yes-no" questions.
10. Pamela was thinking of Cleopatra.
11. She asked if Cleopatra had blond hair.
12. Pamela answered "yes".
13. She should have answered "no".
14. Jenny guessed who it was a few minutes later.
15. Denise told Pamela that Cleopatra had dark hair, not blond hair.
16. Pamela said she didn't care what color her hair was.
17. She called Denise an idiot.
18. Denise never liked to argue or fight.
19. She was tired of Pamela always wanting to be the boss.
20. She called Pamela an idiot, too.
21. She started to go home.
22. Pamela pushed her to the ground and started hitting her.
23. Jenny ran into her house to get her mother.
24. Her mother came out in less than a minute.
25. She separated the two girls.
26. Denise's nose was bleeding.
27. Pamela's dress was torn.
28. She told them to shake hands and to go home.
29. She gave Denise a handkerchief.
30. She gave it to her to stop the bleeding.
31. Pamela called Denise.
32. She called Denise to apologize.
33. Yes, she knew that Pamela had been right about her.
34. Her mother told her.
35. Because Denise had invited her to go to the amusement park on Saturday with some friends and she didn't want to miss the fun.
36. She had invited Pamela the week before.

37. RONNY PERKINS

1. Ronny Perkins lives in Monte Carlo.
2. He lives in a flat.
3. No, he doesn't live in a cheap flat.
4. It costs more money to rent than he earns.
5. Because he always ends up having to ask him for money.
6. He needs a lot of money to maintain the standard of living that he likes.
7. Yes, he owns a yacht.
8. He got the money from his father.
9. He lent it to him.
10. He rents it to people during the summer months.
11. Because the weather is nice in certain months.
12. They cruise around the Gulf of Lyon, all the way to the Balearic Islands.
13. He earns quite a bit of money in the summer.
14. He usually runs out by Christmas.
15. He spends it on fine dinners and lots of drinks.
16. He's well known as a kind of playboy.
17. They don't let him buy on credit.
18. He doesn't know what to do with him.
19. Ronny is already 30 years old.
20. He thinks Ronny isn't going anywhere.
21. Ronny is trying to convince the family to finance the purchase of four yachts.
22. They're from Corsica.
23. He wants to rent two in the Gulf of Lyon and two in the Canary Islands.
24. Because it's summertime all year round there.
25. He's worried about the family from Corsica.
26. He has heard they have connections with the Mafia.
27. He has agreed to lend him $400,000.
28. He'll rent him two other yachts that belong to the family.
29. Nigel doesn't know anything about his son's new business.
30. He has been working on it for over eight months.

Answers

38. MICHAEL JOHNSON

1. He turned 15 last Saturday.
2. He received four presents from his parents.
3. He received three presents from relatives.
4. His father woke him up.
5. He showed him the front page of the sports section in the newspaper.
6. There was a photo of Michael shooting.
7. He was shooting a free throw.
8. It took him about five seconds to wake up completely.
9. He remembered the big game the night before.
10. His middle school team had beaten the Omaha Buffaloes.
11. The final score was 79 to 66.
12. No, his team wasn't favored to win.
13. Michael scored 34 points.
14. He was proud of his son.
15. No, he had never seen Michael play so well.
16. He seemed to control the game.
17. The most important thing for him was that he had held Ricky Tanner to only 12 points.
18. Ricky was the star of the Omaha Buffaloes.
19. Ricky usually scored 36 points a game.
20. Ricky was considered the best young basketball player in the state of Nebraska.
21. He only scored 12 points last night.
22. He followed his coach's advice.
23. His advice was to pay no attention to the ball when playing defense.
24. Michael had the advantage of being faster than Ricky.
25. He concentrated only on Ricky Tanner.
26. The result was suffocating for Ricky and disastrous for his team.

39. PHILLIP JOHNSON

1. Phillip is lying in bed.
2. He's thinking about George Clooney.
3. His wife is in the kitchen washing dishes.
4. She told him about the offer from Eddie Campbell to decorate George Clooney's home in Aspen, Colorado.
5. They had it half an hour ago.
6. No, he's not worried about him.
7. He must be around 50 by now.
8. Most people say that, up close, he isn't that handsome.
9. He's worried that she'll probably start getting other offers of a similar type.
10. A lot of Hollywood stars own homes in Aspen.
11. He could imagine her getting involved in a lot of work up there.
12. Yes, he sees an opportunity in it.
13. He's the general manager.
14. No, he isn't a member of the Board.
15. He can't make the final decision.
16. No, he doesn't feel that he's a real decision-maker.
17. He feels like a glorified employee sometimes.
18. He hates going to Omaha.
19. Because the bank has several difficult clients there and he always has to argue with them about payments.
20. He thinks he might be able to find a job in a bank in Aspen.
21. The town of Aspen is quite big.
22. There are more people there in high season.
23. The population is at its highest in high season.
24. In his opinion, they need bank accounts like everybody else.
25. He thinks he could probably get a job in a local bank.
26. He thinks maybe he could get an even better job in a Denver bank.
27. Denver is three hours from Aspen.
28. Because basketball is even more competitive in Colorado than in Nebraska.
29. He's counting his chickens before they hatch.
30. He has decided to tell her that he supports her one hundred percent.

40. NIGEL PERKINS

1. He has achieved another success.
2. They have just presented proof of a crime.
3. The company asked Nigel's firm to investigate the death of a 62 year-old man.
4. They asked him to investigate it three months ago.
5. He was 62 years old.
6. She was 32 years old.
7. She used to be a model.
8. He died of a heart attack.
9. She received seven million dollars from it.
10. He had been friends with the man.
11. He had personally supervised the investigation of the case.
12. She knew that he suffered from poor blood circulation.
13. She visited nine different pharmacies.
14. She visited them over a period of five months.
15. The drug she bought made his circulation even worse and he died.
16. The medicine was for hemophiliacs.
17. They discovered that she was having an affair with a doctor.
18. The woman lived in a flat.
19. They went through garbage in the building where she lived.
20. The garbage was in the basement of the building.
21. They searched through at least one ton of garbage.
22. They finally found a prescription in the garbage for the medicine in question.
23. It took them ten days.
24. The name of the doctor she was having an affair with was on it.
25. They contacted the distributors of the medicine.
26. They visited 27 pharmacies.
27. They visited pharmacies in the general area where the woman lived.
28. Employees in four different pharmacies recognized her from a photograph.
29. They contacted the police after that.
30. The police interrogated the woman first.
31. She denied everything.
32. They interrogated the doctor next.
33. He confessed to the crime.
34. They are in prison now.
35. They're awaiting trial.
36. Six of the seven million dollars have been recovered.

41. AKI MORITA

1. He feels relieved.
2. He has just given his wife news about their transfer to Louisiana.
3. He told her ten minutes ago.
4. He expected the news to be bad.
5. They hardly ever talk about his work.
6. Because they hardly ever have time to talk to each other.
7. They talked for at least 15 minutes.
8. He was surprised because his wife knew more about Louisiana than he did.
9. She knows 10 times more about it than he does.
10. She knew about Baton Rouge, New Orleans and Natchez.
11. The plantation homes are located here.
12. She spends a lot of time reading.
13. She read it three months ago.
14. It was about a rich Louisiana family before and during the American Civil War.
15. She explained the history and way of life in Louisiana during that period.
16. He couldn't believe it.
17. He told her they would probably spend three years there.
18. No, she wasn't upset.
19. She thought it would be a good opportunity for the children.
20. Because they could learn English well.
21. She had heard that Japanese families who are transferred to Europe or America lead a very good life.
22. It is almost double.
23. Because they receive a special allowance.
24. Because she reads at least four American novels every year.
25. She has a romantic vision of it.

42. INÉS GARCÍA

1. She's in Seville today.
2. It's her first day back there.
3. She was in Paris.
4. She was there for four days.
5. She spent the four days with François Monet.
6. She had been there once before.
7. She went there when she was a little girl.
8. She only remembered the Eiffel Tower and Notre Dame from that visit.
9. He took her to all the popular sights and to several charming places.
10. The highlight was the hour she spent in a rowboat with François in the Boulogne Forest.
11. It's just outside of Paris.
12. The weather was lovely.
13. They had a lovely time.
14. She returned on Sunday.
15. He told her he was falling in love.
16. She didn't say anything to him.
17. She didn't want him to know that she was absolutely crazy about him.
18. She made the decision to break up with him.
19. She made it on the flight back to Seville.
20. She decided that she would tell him everything.
21. She thought it would be hard for him.
22. They had been together for four years.
23. She considered their relationship to be fun but not passionate.
24. No, she hadn't ever met anyone like him.
25. She was experiencing a feeling she had never known before.
26. She was convinced she had finally met Mr. Right.

43. PAULA EISENBACH

1. She's glad she has only one more semester before she finishes her studies.
2. She loves Heidelberg but wants to get away from it.
3. She's sunbathing on a long beach in the Canary Islands.
4. She's with her parents.
5. Her last two weeks there were unbearable.
6. He has been calling her.
7. He calls her at least three times a day.
8. She has seen him following her.
9. She has seen him following her twice.
10. She has seen him following her between the university buildings.
11. They told her she should call the police.
12. She doesn't think it's necessary.
13. She thinks he'll eventually get over his infatuation with her.
14. She may go to the police.
15. She'll get back there in January.
16. He's a strange man.
17. He's a very talented one.
18. He's extremely introverted.
19. He works on his drawings and talks about how he hates the food in Germany.
20. It's always messy.
21. He always wears the same blue suit without a tie, or a Disneyland T-shirt.
22. He never goes out.
23. He doesn't seem to have any friends.
24. She worked at his apartment for about two months.
25. He never asked her out to dinner.
26. They never went out for a coffee.
27. She can forget about Tom and enjoy the sun and the beach.
28. She'll go to Munich with her parents.
29. She'll be there for another week.
30. She'll go to Heidelberg.
31. She hopes he'll have found another person to help him.
32. She hopes he'll have forgotten about her.

44. PIERRE MONET

1. He had to stay there until 7:00 p.m.
2. He was asked to work.
3. He was asked to work with a colleague to translate a secret document.
4. It arrived just before 4:00 p.m.
5. It arrived from the French Embassy in London.
6. He usually goes home at 4:00.
7. His boss asked him to stay longer.
8. No, he didn't walk calmly into his office.
9. He rushed into his office.
10. He was getting ready to leave.
11. The President of the Republic needed the document translated.
12. He needed it immediately.
13. He called his wife.
14. He told her that he would be late.
15. She told him that he had just received a report from the Chairman of Peugeot.
16. It needed to be done by 9:00 a.m. the next morning.
17. He told her he would be home around 8:00 p.m.
18. He told her he would probably need no more than two hours to do it.
19. It was 15 pages long.
20. It was 23 pages long.
21. He divided it up with a colleague.
22. He wondered how it had found its way to the French Embassy.
23. It was really none of his business.
24. It was from the British Ministry of Defense.
25. It was addressed to the Prime Minister.
26. It was about the British position concerning the construction of a new Eurofighter attack jet.
27. The U.K., France, Germany and Spain were involved in its construction.
28. He complained about the French and the Germans.
29. His complaint was that the U.K. and Spain weren't being included in some of the sensitive meetings and decisions.
30. It contained a list of meetings that had taken place between the French and German companies without the knowledge of the other two partners.
31. The Minister recommended that the subject of the meetings between the French and German companies be included in the next meeting.
32. It was scheduled during the next NATO meeting.
33. It was supposed to be an informal meeting.
34. It was going to take place in Brussels.
35. Because Brussels was the location for the next NATO meeting.

45. NATASHA ZARAKOVICH

1. She's in Scotland now.
2. She thought she knew English well.
3. Her first two days in Scotland have made her think otherwise.
4. She arrived on Friday the twenty-second.
5. She spent Saturday and Sunday with her cousin, André, and his family.
6. In the evenings she went out with André and a group of friends.
7. No, she didn't have any trouble understanding them.
8. Because they spoke Russian or English with a slight accent.
9. She had trouble understanding André's friends.
10. She had to make a big effort.
11. The fact that they went to a noisy restaurant and then to a discotheque made things worse.
12. She felt embarrassed because she kept having to ask the friends to repeat.
13. André told her not to worry about it.
14. He thought that she would understand everyone quite well by the time she left for Moscow.
15. She would leave for Moscow in early January.
16. He took her to Edinburgh.
17. It's the capital of Scotland.
18. She had never seen such a beautiful city.
19. She was standing in Princes Street for more than half an hour.
20. She spent so much time there because she was looking across at the castle of Mary, Queen of Scots.
21. The weather was cold and windy.
22. He wanted to go inside a pub to get warm.
23. No, she didn't feel cold.
24. Because she was used to the Russian winters.
25. She found that things were so different compared to Moscow.
26. She had never been more than 50 kilometers outside of Moscow.
27. She saw cars everywhere.
28. The people all seemed to be in a hurry.
29. He said that Edinburgh and Glasgow were quiet cities compared to it.
30. He said they would be going there in a few days.
31. They would see the sights and go to a musical.
32. They would either see "Cats" or "The Phantom of the Opera".

46. LI TONG

1. He was thinking about giving up the idea of learning English.

2. He had already attended six classes.

3. He still couldn't understand a word the teacher was saying.

4. He felt embarrassed there.

5. Because most of the students seemed to be progressing quite well.

6. He had the impression that he was holding back the class.

7. Thanks to his daughter, he changed it.

8. He talked to his wife about it.

9. His daughter heard him tell her.

10. She was doing her homework.

11. She was doing it at the kitchen table.

12. She got up and told him that English was easy.

13. She showed him her English book.

14. They studied the first two chapters together.

15. Li had always thought that his daughter was a gifted child.

16. He was now sure that she was gifted.

17. She explained to him how to conjugate the verb 'to be' in the singular, plural and first, second and third person.

18. She asked him questions using the interrogative form of 'to be'.

19. He was impressed.

20. She is only eight years old.

21. She was teaching English better than his English teacher.

22. They practiced them for over 30 minutes.

23. He made the resolution to continue studying the language.

24. He made it that night when he went to bed.

47. ANNA BARGHINI

1. Anna is on her way to Stuttgart.
2. She's going there by plane.
3. She's flying business class.
4. She's thinking about Karl Polster.
5. She never thought she would like a German man.
6. She received a letter from Karl.
7. Yes, he told her his true feelings in it.
8. It was only three paragraphs long.
9. He must have spent hours writing it.
10. It made a strong and pleasant impression on her.
11. He told her that he wasn't the type of person to insinuate his feelings to anyone.
12. He admitted that he was very fond of her.
13. He said he couldn't stop thinking about her.
14. He said she was one of the most attractive and intelligent women he had ever met.
15. He had been deeply affected by her presence.
16. He said he knew that her family was wealthy.
17. He assured her that money was not, and had never been, a factor that influenced his feelings toward people.
18. His family was upper middle class and had a small, but comfortable estate.
19. He said that he was not ambitious to amass a fortune.
20. He asked her to have dinner with him.
21. He invited her to a small restaurant in the center of town.
22. His uncle owns the restaurant.
23. It serves Alsatian cuisine.
24. It serves the best Alsatian cuisine he has ever tasted.
25. She sat still for a moment after reading it.
26. She had never received such a warm, sincere letter in her life.
27. She decided that maybe she ought to get to know this fellow a little better.

48. NANCY JOHNSON

1. They took Friday off.
2. They took it off to drive to Denver.
3. They drove across Nebraska and half of Colorado.
4. It took them nine hours.
5. They stayed at the Marriot Hotel.
6. They drove to Aspen the next morning.
7. They're endless, winding roads.
8. They had lunch in Aspen.
9. Nancy took the car after lunch.
10. She drove to the house George Clooney had bought.
11. She saw a man when she got there.
12. He was holding a shovel.
13. He was clearing a path to the front door.
14. No, he didn't see her arrive.
15. She asked him if Mr. Clooney was in.
16. She scared him because he hadn't heard her come up to him from behind.
17. He smiled and said "yes".
18. The man was George Clooney.
19. She froze.
20. She had thought the man was a gardener or someone similar.
21. She could only manage to say her name.
22. He was used to this kind of reaction.
23. He invited her into the house to have a coffee.
24. She realized that no one had lived there for a long time.
25. The house was cold, dirty and empty.
26. They went into the kitchen.
27. Because Mr. Clooney had an electric heater on.
28. He poured two coffees.
29. They sat down at an old wooden table.
30. 30. The problem was that one of the legs was shorter than the other three.
31. She didn't notice it because she was thinking about her hair and her clothes.
32. He was wearing a pair of old blue jeans and a flannel shirt.

49. LUIGI BARGHINI

1. He's in Verona.
2. He's escorting three engineers from Mercedes Benz around his factory.
3. He's showing them the different steps in the manufacturing process.
4. He, Anna, and the Technical Director of the company had a meeting with the engineers.
5. Six people attended the meeting.
6. Luigi, Anna and the Technical Director attended from Luigi's company.
7. They went over every detail of a supply agreement.
8. He described the raw materials used in making the car seats and the aluminum used in the frames.
9. She spoke about the company's fine record in deliveries and in quality assurance.
10. Luigi explained how the car seats would be shipped to Stuttgart.
11. He's the Chief Engineer from Mercedes.
12. He didn't seem convinced.
13. He was worried about strikes that could delay shipments and cause production problems in Germany.
14. Anna assured him that the company had suffered only one strike.
15. It was a general strike throughout Italy.
16. It had lasted only two days.
17. She explained that the workers were paid well above the going rate in the area and in the automotive industry.
18. He added that he spent a lot of time with the workers and was proud of the spirit and collaboration on the factory floor.
19. He showed them four different awards the company had received from different customers.
20. They were for the quality of their work.
21. Two of them were from Fiat.
22. Volvo and Rover had also given them an award.
23. He looked at them but didn't say anything.

50. RONNY PERKINS

1. He's concerned about his new business.

2. He acquired three new yachts.

3. The Turqui family helped him.

4. He has four yachts in all.

5. He operates two yachts in the Gulf of Lyon.

6. He has started operations in the Canary Islands.

7. He has two yachts there.

8. He doesn't trust the Turqui family.

9. He especially doesn't trust Giuseppe's son, Carlo.

10. The original agreement was to give Ronny a loan to buy one yacht and to rent him two more.

11. The family ended up giving him all three yachts in exchange for 50 percent of his company.

12. They acquired 50 percent of the business.

13. Because he wasn't in a position to negotiate.

14. Carlo is talking about increasing the capital of the company.

15. He wants to use it to buy eight new yachts to expand the business even more.

16. It would amount to over three million dollars.

17. He won't have enough money to maintain his 50% share of the business.

18. He thinks the family is going to gradually take over his company.

19. He sent a member of his private investigation agency to Monte Carlo and Corsica.

20. He sent him there one month ago.

21. No, Ronny doesn't know about it.

22. He told him to look into the Turqui family and Ronny's finances as well.

23. No, Ronny had never mentioned the Turqui family to Nigel.

24. He found out about it through a friend of his in the London offices of Barclay's Bank, who had heard about it from the manager of Barclay's operations in Monaco.

51. AKI MORITA

1. They've been there for two months.
2. No, he hasn't changed his habits.
3. He leaves home befor 7:00 a.m.
4. He gets back home just before dinner time.
5. People have dinner at 6:00 p.m. in Louisiana.
6. They still have dinner around 8:00.
7. The new Honda factory was three months away from completion when he arrived.
8. It's on schedule.
9. Production should start within six weeks.
10. He's busy making contacts with suppliers and training the factory personnel.
11. He needs more people in his department.
12. He needs them to evaluate the American suppliers who are bidding on supply contracts.
13. He's in charge of purchasing.
14. He has the advantage of living in the States for two years and knowing more about how things work.
15. His English is improving tremendously.
16. He's finally starting to understand the strange southern accent spoken by the people in Louisiana.
17. She's enjoying her new life for the moment.
18. She has made friends with the purchasing manager's wife.
19. She's American.
20. She's from a small town in Texas called Bertram.
21. She wants to learn Japanese.
22. She has agreed to give her classes.
23. She is going to give her the classes for free.
24. They both live on the same block.
25. They always go shopping together.
26. She loves to shop at the nearby mall.
27. It's not far from her house.
28. She thinks there must be more than 200 different shops there.
29. She doesn't think the prices are bad.
30. Aki earns almost double what he earned in Japan.
31. The only problem seems to be the kids.
32. The biggest problem is the language barrier.
33. They're young and they'll soon learn to speak English.

52. PHILLIP JOHNSON

1. He feels like the queen's consort.

2. She has only been involved with the house for three weeks.

3. Because her picture was on the front page of the local newspaper.

4. It was published the day after the news got out.

5. Everyone is comparing her to Demi Moore in the movie "Indecent Proposal".

6. Redford paid Demi Moore a million dollars to spend the night with him.

7. He doesn't appreciate the jokes.

8. He likes the idea that she is earning almost a quarter of a million dollars.

9. She'll be involved in it for eight months.

10. He only sees her on Mondays and Tuesdays.

11. Because weekends are the only time George Clooney can get away from Los Angeles.

12. She lives in Aspen.

13. She's renting one.

14. She has set up her design studio in it.

15. He's a delightful person.

16. He has good taste for decoration.

17. He leaves most of the decisions up to her.

18. He isn't a jealous person by nature.

19. He's concerned that working closely with George Clooney would be any woman's dream.

20. He's starting to feel that it's more and more tedious.

21. He has bought a subscription to the Denver Post.

22. He is looking for some decent job offers.

23. He hasn't seen any so far.

24. He talks with her every night.

25. They're about half an hour long.

26. He thinks it's going to be very high.

27. Because there are a lot of nice things the family can do with $250,000.

53. INÉS GARCÍA

1. She had never been so excited in her life.
2. She returned from Paris two months ago.
3. She had talked to him on the phone almost every day.
4. He usually called her.
5. Because otherwise, her father might have said something to her about the phone bill.
6. He surprised her with some unbelievable news.
7. He had spoken to his uncle about her.
8. He had mentioned her to him a week earlier.
9. Pierre is François's uncle.
10. He told Pierre he was looking for a way to bring Inés to live in Paris.
11. He called François.
12. He asked the Chairman if they might need a lawyer expert in Spanish law.
13. He said no.
14. He went on to explain the circumstances.
15. He said his nephew was love-sick.
16. His benevolent side came out when Pierre told him about his nephew.
17. He assured Pierre that Inés could come to work for Peugeot.
18. She jumped for joy.
19. She was tired of defending boring labor cases.
20. She was dying to see François.
21. He told her to prepare her CV.
22. No, he didn't tell her to send it to him.
23. He told her to send it to the Chairman of Peugeot.
24. He told her to write a letter.
25. He told her to thank the Chairman for his fine gesture and to say something about herself.
26. She called a friend of hers who had grown up in France.
27. She asked if she could help her write a letter and a CV in French.
28. She sent them two days later.
29. She got a reply seven days later.
30. It was from the head of Human Resources.
31. He offered her an initial one-year contract.
32. She would work as an assistant to the Chief Legal Counsel.
33. He told her that she should be ready to work within 30 days.
34. It was a dream come true for her.
35. Her father thought it was wonderful.
36. Her mother insisted on meeting François first.
37. He immediately reserved an airplane ticket.
38. He reserved it with Iberia.
39. He would fly the Paris-Madrid-Seville route.
40. He would be there the following weekend.

54. KARL POLSTER

1. He was sitting opposite Anna Barghini.
2. They were having dinner in a small, intimate restaurant.
3. It was in the center of Stuttgart.
4. Karl had "opened his heart" to Anna in it.
5. He had sent it to her the week before.
6. He felt self-conscious and unsure of himself.
7. She was rich and beautiful.
8. He was impressed even more that she was only 27.
9. One could say that they were the result of having a rich father who owned a company.
10. One would have to admit that her beauty was hers and hers alone.
11. She had won the respect of a lot of people at Mercedes.
12. Because she had a keen business sense.
13. He wanted to gain her affection.
14. He couldn't keep from feeling nervous.
15. Yes, he was older than her.
16. He was 34 years old.
17. It had been 7 years since he had had a serious relationship with a woman.
18. He had been engaged to a girl from Hanover.
19. She died in a traffic accident.
20. It happened two months before they were supposed to be married.
21. He had had no relationships with any women since then.
22. He hat devoted himself entirely to his job at Mercedes.
23. He was now the General Purchasing Director.
24. He realized that it had changed his personality and made him a much more serious person.
25. He was having trouble relating to Anna in a fun, natural way.
26. He told her about the tragic events of seven years ago.
27. She said very little during most of the meal.
28. She felt comfortable and at ease with him.
29. He seemed like a sad person who was trying his best to be a pleasant host.
30. She thought he seemed sincere and she could see that he was very cultured.

55. MICHAEL JOHNSON

1. He turned 15.
2. He's studying at high school.
3. High school is where students do the last four years of secondary education before going to university.
4. In some states, it's the last three years of secondary education.
5. He's in a 4-year high school.
6. He's one of the youngest in the school.
7. Most of them seem a lot older and more mature.
8. The school has two basketball teams.
9. He has started practicing with the senior team.
10. It isn't a problem.
11. He's 1 meter, 81 centimeters tall.
12. He saw him play in three games last year.
13. He was in middle school.
14. Yes, he saw him in the state finals.
15. He scored 34 points and held Ricky Tanner to only 12 points.
16. Because he was really impressed by his performance against Ricky Tanner.
17. He's sure that by the time Michael turns 17, he could become one of the best high school players in the nation.
18. Because he has never seen a boy so good in every aspect of the game.
19. He's one of the boys competing for the position of point guard.
20. Four, including Michael, are competing for it.
21. He's definitely better than two of them.
22. He's an excellent shot and never misses a basket.
23. His average was 18 points a game.
24. He played on the senior team.
25. He's faster and probably much better on defense.
26. He thinks the coach could move Dennis to another position.
27. He has made the decision to start Dennis in the first two games and send in Michael in the second half.
28. He'll move him down to the junior team for this season.

Phillip Johnson

Michael Johnson

Denise Johnson

Nigel Perkins

Luigi Barghini

Pierre Monet

Paula Eisenbach

Li Tong

Aki Morita

Natasha Zarakovich

Inés García

Richard Vaughan